The Original
Summer Bridge Activities™
Fourth to Fifth Grade

SBA was created by
Michele D. Van Leeuwen

written by
Julia Ann Hobbs
Carla Dawn Fisher

illustrations by
Magen Mitchell
Amanda Sorensen

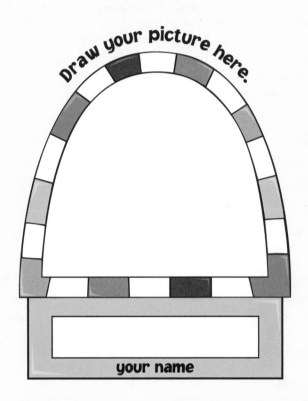

Draw your picture here.

your name

Summer Learning Staff
Clareen Arnold, Lori Davis, Melody Feist, Aimee Hansen, Christopher Kugler, Kristina Kugler, Molly McMahon, Paul Rawlins, Liza Richards, Linda Swain

Design
Andy Carlson, Robyn Funk

Cover Art
Karen Maizel, Amanda Sorensen

ISBN: 978-1-59441-730-6

Super Summer Science pages © 2002 The Wild Goose Company and Carson-Dellosa.

20 19 18 17 16 15 14 13 12 11

Dear Parents,

The summer months are a perfect time to reconnect with your child on many levels after a long school year. Your personal involvement is so important to your child's immediate and long-term academic success. No matter how wonderful your child's classroom experience is, your involvement outside the classroom will make it that much better!

Summer Bridge Activities™ is the original summer workbook developed to help parents support their children academically while away from school, and we strive to improve the content, the activities, and the resources to give you the highest quality summer learning materials available. Ten years ago, we introduced Summer Bridge Activities™ to a small group of teachers and parents after I had successfully used it to help my first grader prepare for the new school year. It was a hit then, and it continues to be a hit now! Many other summer workbooks have been introduced since, but Summer Bridge Activities™ continues to be the one that both teachers and parents ask for most. We take our responsibility as the leader in summer education seriously and are always looking for new ways to make summer learning more fun, more motivating, and more effective to help make your child's transition to the new school year enjoyable and successful!

We are now excited to offer you even more bonus summer learning materials online at www.SummerBridgeActivities.com! This site has great resources for both parents and kids to use on their own and together. An expanded summer reading program where kids can post their own book reviews, writing and reading contests with great prizes, assessment tests, travel packs, and even games are just a few of the additional resources that you and your child will have access to with the included Summer Bridge Activities™ Online Pass Code.

Summer Learning has come a long way over the last 10 years, and we are glad that you have chosen to use Summer Bridge Activities™ to help your children continue to discover the world around them by using the classroom skills they worked so hard to obtain!

Have a wonderful summer!

Michele Van Leeuwen and the Summer Learning Staff!

Hey Kids!

We bet you had a great school year!
Congratulations on all your hard work! We just want to say
that we're proud of the great things you did this year, and we're excited
to have you spend time with us over the summer. Have fun with your
Summer Bridge Activities™ workbook, and visit us online at
www.SummerBridgeActivities.com for more fun, cool, and exciting stuff!

Have a great summer!

The T. O. C. (Table of Contents)

Official Pass Code

kk0731r

Log on to www.SummerBridgeActivities.com and join!

Sections of SBA

 There are three sections in SBA: the first and second review, the third previews.

 Each section begins with an SBA Motivational Calendar.

 Each day your child will complete an activity in reading, writing, math, and language. The activities become progressively more challenging.

 Each page is numbered by day.

Here's what you will find inside

Summer Bridge Activities™

Exercises in **Summer Bridge Activities™** (SBA) are easy to understand and presented in fun and creative ways that motivate children to review familiar skills while being progressively challenged. In addition to basic skills in reading, writing, math, and language arts, SBA contains activities that challenge and reinforce skills in geography and science!

Daily exercises review and preview skills in reading, writing, math, and language arts, with additional activities in geography and science. Activities are presented in half-page increments so kids do not get overwhelmed and are divided into three sections to correlate with traditional summer vacation.

Bonus Super Summer Science pages provide hands-on science activities.

A Summer Reading List introduces kids to some of today's popular titles as well as the classics. Kids can rate books they read and log on to www.**SummerBridgeActivities**.com to post reviews, find more great titles, and participate in national reading and writing contests!

Motivational Calendars begin each section and help kids achieve all summer long.

Discover Something New lists offer fun and creative activities that teach kids with their hands and get them active and learning.

Grade-specific flashcards provide a great way to reinforce basic skills in addition to the written exercises.

Removable Answer Pages ensure that parents know as much as their kids!

A Certificate of Completion for parents to sign congratulates kids for their work and welcomes them to the grade ahead.

A grade-appropriate, official Summer Fun pass code gives kids and parents online access to more bonus games, contests, and resources at www.**SummerBridgeActivities**.com.

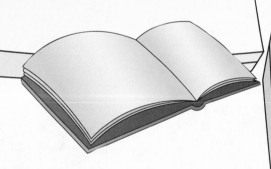

Here are some groups who say our books are great!

Mr. Fredrickson

10 Ways to Maximize
The Original Summer Bridge Activities™

1. First, let your child explore the book. Flip through the pages and look at the activities with your child to help him become familiar with the book.

2. Help select a good time for reading or working on the activities. Suggest a time before your child has played outside and becomes too tired to do the work.

3. Provide any necessary materials. A pencil, ruler, eraser, or reference works may be required.

4. Offer positive guidance. Remember, the activities are not meant to be tests. You want to create a relaxed and positive attitude toward learning. Work through at least one example on each page with your child. "Think aloud" and show your child how to solve problems.

5. Give your child plenty of time to think. You may be surprised by how much children can do on their own.

6. Stretch your child's thinking beyond the page. If you are reading a book, you might ask, "What do you think will happen next?" or "What would you do if this happened to you?" Encourage your child to talk about her interests and observations about the world around her.

7. Reread stories and occasionally flip through completed pages. Completed pages and books will be a source of pride to your child and will help show how much he accomplished over the summer.

8. Read and work on activities while outside. Take the workbook out in the backyard or on a family campout. It can be fun wherever you are!

9. Encourage siblings, relatives, and neighborhood friends to help with reading and activities. Other children are often perfect for providing the one-on-one attention necessary to reinforce reading skills.

10. Give plenty of approval! Stickers and stamps are effective for recognizing a job well done. At the end of the summer, your child can feel proud of her accomplishments and will be eager for school to start.

Skills List

Language Arts/Reading

- [ ] Is able to complete analogies
- [ ] Recognizes compound words
- [ ] Recognizes contractions
- [ ] Recognizes antonyms, synonyms, and homonyms
- [ ] Recognizes tenses of verbs
- [ ] Recognizes parts of speech
- [ ] Uses correct punctuation
- [ ] Recognizes complete and incomplete sentences
- [ ] Uses possessives properly
- [ ] Can identify the main idea from context clues in a story
- [ ] Can identify the setting of a story
- [ ] Can identify the conflict of a story
- [ ] Can identify the conclusion of a story
- [ ] Can identify cause and effect relationships in a story
- [ ] Can make predictions from content clues
- [ ] Can identify common abbreviations
- [ ] Uses the writing and editing process correctly
- [ ] Can use a dictionary and encyclopedia
- [ ] Can identify prefixes and suffixes
- [ ] Is able to construct a short story
- [ ] Is able to write a friendly letter
- [ ] Reads and writes for pleasure
- [ ] Recognizes literary genres: poetry, nonfiction, tall tales, etc.
- [ ] Can properly address an envelope

Parent:

Exercises for these skills can be found inside **Summer Bridge Activities™** and can be used for extra practice. The skills lists are a great way to discover your child's strengths or what skills may need additional reinforcement.

Skills List

Math

- [ ] Recognizes numbers to 9,999,999
- [ ] Can identify 2- and 3-dimensional geometric shapes
- [ ] Can read and interpret a graph
- [ ] Understands place value up to the millions place
- [ ] Is able to use decimals to the hundredths place
- [ ] Can recall all addition facts (sums to 24)
- [ ] Can recall all subtraction facts (subtrahends: 0–10)
- [ ] Can recall all multiplication facts (factors: 0–12)
- [ ] Can recall all division facts (divisors: 1–9)
- [ ] Performs 4-digit addition with regrouping
- [ ] Performs 4-digit subtraction with regrouping
- [ ] Can make estimations
- [ ] Can count money to make change
- [ ] Can perform money addition problems using a decimal point
- [ ] Can perform money subtraction problems using a decimal point
- [ ] Can tell time by the minute
- [ ] Can measure using standard units and the metric system
- [ ] Can order fractions
- [ ] Can find equivalent fractions
- [ ] Can subtract fractions
- [ ] Can perform money multiplication problems using a decimal point
- [ ] Can perform money division using a decimal point
- [ ] Uses problem-solving strategies to complete math problems

Summertime = Reading Time!

We all know how important reading is, but this summer show kids how GREAT the adventures of reading really are! Summer learning and summer reading go hand-in-hand, so here are a few ideas to get you up and going:

Encourage your child to read out loud to you and make a theatrical performance out of even the smallest and simplest read. Have fun with reading and impress the family at the campsite next to you at the same time!

Establish a time to read together each day. Make sure and ask each other about what you are reading and try to relate it to something that may be going on within the family.

Show off! Let your child see you reading for enjoyment and talk about the great things that you are discovering from what you read. Laugh out loud, stamp your feet—it's summertime!

Sit down with your child and establish a summer reading program. Use our cool Summer Reading List and Summer Reading Program at www.**SummerBridgeActivities**.com, or visit your local bookstore and, of course, your local library. Encourage your child to select books on topics he is interested in and on his reading level. A rule of thumb for selecting books at the appropriate reading level is to choose a page and have your child read it out loud. If he doesn't know five or more of the words on the page, the book may be too difficult.

Use your surroundings (wherever you are) to show your child how important reading is on a daily basis. Read newspaper articles, magazines, stories, and road maps during the family vacation...just don't get lost!

Find books that tie into your child's experiences. If you are going fishing or boating, find a book on the subject to share. This will help your child learn and develop interests in new things.

Get library cards! Set a regular time to visit the library and encourage your child to have her books read and ready to return so she is ready for the next adventure! Let your child choose her own books. It will encourage her to read and pursue her own interests.

Make up your own stories! This is great fun and can be done almost anywhere—in the car, on camping trips, in a canoe, on a plane! Encourage your child to tell the story with a beginning, middle, AND end! To really challenge each other, start with the end, then middle, and then the beginning— yikes!

Books to Read

The Summer Reading List has a variety of titles, including some found in the Accelerated Reader Program.

We recommend parents read to pre-kindergarten through 1st grade children 5–10 minutes each day and then ask questions about the story to reinforce comprehension. For higher grade levels, we suggest the following daily reading times: grades 1–2, 10–20 min.; grades 2–3, 20–30 min.; grades 3–4, 30–45 min.; grades 4–6, 45–60 min.

It is important to decide an amount of reading time and write it on the SBA Motivational Calendar.

Summer Bridge Activities™
Summer Reading List

Fill in the stars and rate your favorite (and not so favorite) books here and online at
www.SummerBridgeActivities.com!

1 = I struggled to finish this book.
2 = I thought this book was pretty good.
3 = I thought this book rocked!
4 = I want to read this book again and again!

Frindle ☆☆☆☆

Clements, Andrew

Chasing Redbird ☆☆☆☆

Creech, Sharon

Gone-Away Lake ☆☆☆☆

Enright, Elizabeth

Join Portia, Foster, and Julian for their enchanted summer as they discover the hidden wonders of a summer retreat whose residents have dwindled to two—elderly Minnehaha Cheever and her brother, Pindar Payton.

Fourth Graders Don't Believe in Witches ☆☆☆☆

Fields, Terri

The Whipping Boy ☆☆☆☆

Fleischman, Sid

Stone Fox ☆☆☆☆

Gardiner, John R.

Lily's Crossing ☆☆☆☆

Giff, Patricia R.

The Reluctant Dragon ☆☆☆☆

Graham, Kenneth

Good-Bye, My Wishing Star ☆☆☆☆

Grove, Vicki

Time for Andrew: A Ghost Story ☆☆☆☆

Hahn, Mary Downing

Who knew that finding a bag of marbles under the attic floorboards could change two boys' lives forever? A thrilling tale of time travel and intrigue.

Rabbit Hill ☆☆☆☆☆

Lawson, Robert

Island of the Blue Dolphins ☆☆☆☆☆

O'Dell, Scott

Strawberry Girl ☆☆☆☆☆

Lenski, Lois

Mick Harte Was Here ☆☆☆☆☆

Park, Barbara

Chocolate Covered Ants ☆☆☆☆☆

Manes, Stephanie

Poison Ivy and Eyebrow Wigs ☆☆☆☆☆

Pryor, Bonnie

The Kid Who Named Pluto ☆☆☆☆☆

McCutcheon, Marc

Holes ☆☆☆☆☆

Sachar, Louis

This book showcases the work and lives of nine people who were very young when they began making significant contributions to science. Who named Pluto? That would be 11-year-old Venetia Burney.

Knights of the Kitchen Table ☆☆☆☆☆

Scieszka, Jon

Series of Unfortunate Events ☆☆☆☆☆

Snicket, Lemony

The Rag Coat ☆☆☆☆☆

Mills, Lauren A.

Orphan Train Rider: One Boy's True Story ☆☆☆☆☆

Warren, Andrea

Owls in the Family ☆☆☆☆☆

Mowat, Farley

Stepbrother Sabotage ☆☆☆☆☆

Wittman, Sally

Join the SBA Kids Summer Reading Club!

Quick! Get Mom or Dad to help you log on and join the SBA Kids Summer Reading Club. You can find more great books, tell your friends about your favorite titles, and even win cool prizes! Log on to www.SummerBridgeActivities.com and sign up today.

Book cover from THE KID WHO NAMED PLUTO AND THE STORIES OF OTHER EXTRAORDINARY YOUNG PEOPLE IN SCIENCE by Marc McCutcheon, Illustrated by Jon Cannell. (c) 2005. Published by Chronicle Books, LLC.

Summer Bridge Activities™

Motivational Calendar

Month _____

My parents and I decided that if I complete
15 days of **Summer Bridge Activities**™ and
read _____ minutes a day, my incentive/reward will be:

_____

Child's Signature _____ Parent's Signature _____

Day 1	☆	📖	_____	Day 9	☆	📖	_____
Day 2	☆	📖	_____	Day 10	☆	📖	_____
Day 3	☆	📖		Day 11	☆	📖	_____
Day 4	☆	📖	_____	Day 12	☆	📖	_____
Day 5	☆	📖		Day 13	☆	📖	_____
Day 6	☆	📖	_____	Day 14	☆	📖	_____
Day 7	☆	📖	_____	Day 15	☆	📖	_____
Day 8	☆	📖					

Child: Color the ☆ for daily activities completed.
Color the 📖 for daily reading completed.

Parent: Initial the _____ when all activities are complete.

1

Discover Something New!

1 Describe what you look like and write it down.

2 Polish a pair of your mom's or dad's shoes and put a love note in the toe.

3 Visit a sick neighbor, friend, or relative.

4 In the evening, look at the sky. Find the first star and make a wish.

5 Pick one of your favorite foods and learn how to make it.

6 Make a picnic lunch for two; then invite a friend over and have a picnic in your backyard.

Fun Activity Ideas to Go Along with Section One!

7 Start a diary.

8 Ask your mom or dad for an old map and plan a trip. Decide on a destination and highlight your route. Figure out how many days it would take, where you would stop, and what you would like to see. Use the legend on the map to help you make these decisions.

9 Hold a fire drill in your home.

10 Find some old socks, buttons, yarn, and needle and thread. Make puppets and name them. Then find a cardboard box and paint it. Cut a hole in the front to put the puppets through and put on a puppet show for younger children.

11 Feed the birds.

12 Learn how to do something you have always wanted to do, like play the guitar, cross-stitch, rollerblade, cook pizza, train your dog, etc.

13 Have a watermelon bust.

14 Write a story about your friend.

15 Make a pitcher of lemonade or tropical Kool-Aid and sell it in front of your house.

Mixed Skills Practice. Watch the operation signs.

1. 13 − 5 = _____

2. 9 + 2 = _____

3. 6 x 5 = _____

4. 17 − 9 = _____

5. 1 x 2 = _____

6. 15 − 9 = _____

7. 0 ÷ 3 = _____

8. 10 ÷ 2 = _____

9. 30 ÷ 6 = _____

10. 3 x 6 = _____

11. 4 x 3 = _____

12. 6 + 9 = _____

13. 6 + 4 = _____

14. 13 + 5 = _____

15. 27 ÷ 3 = _____

16. 20 ÷ 4 = _____

17. 6 − 0 = _____

18. 9 x 7 = _____

Find the missing number.

19. 18 ÷ ☐ = 6

20. ☐ ÷ 4 = 8

21. ☐ + 6 = 12

22. 5 + ☐ = 6

23. 3 x ☐ = 21

24. 4 x ☐ = 36

25. 10 − ☐ = 3

26. ☐ ÷ 6 = 4

27. ☐ − 6 = 7

28. 24 ÷ ☐ = 3

29. ☐ + 4 = 9

30. ☐ x 7 = 0

Write <u>yes</u> before each group of words that make a sentence. Write <u>no</u> if the group is not a sentence. (<u>Remember</u>: A sentence is a group of words that express a complete thought.)

_____ 1. Tom carried the canned food.

_____ 2. Will you feed the pets?

_____ 3. Butterflies have beautiful.

_____ 4. Don't forget to call me.

_____ 5. For his tenth birthday.

_____ 6. Wrapped the gift.

_____ 7. Turtles have hard shells.

_____ 8. We will turn to page.

_____ 9. Everyone enjoyed the trip.

_____ 10. Ants are insects.

_____ 11. Have you fastened?

_____ 12. Do you have hiking boots?

_____ 13. Wash your hands before.

_____ 14. Cats are furry.

A <u>thesaurus</u> is a reference book that contains synonyms and antonyms. In each row below, circle the word that <u>does not</u> belong. (Use a thesaurus if needed.)

1. maxim saying pledge proverb
2. folk tribe clan enemy
3. time moon globe satellite
4. notice overlook observe see
5. daystar sun orb planet
6. leader follower first alpha
7. mention remark play comment
8. goose pig duck swan

Seek and Find. The telephone book is a reference book. There is a lot of useful information in a telephone book.

The <u>White Pages</u> list people's names and telephone numbers in alphabetical order by last name.

The <u>Yellow Pages</u> list businesses' telephone numbers by type of business. <u>Emergency</u> information is in the front of the book.

1. Find a friend's name and number in the telephone book and write it down.

   _____

2. Look up and list the phone numbers that would be helpful to you in case of an emergency.

   _____

   _____

3. Find your school's phone number. _____

4. Look up your favorite restaurant's phone number. _____

5. Look up the phone numbers of your favorite places to go. _____

   _____

   _____

Add or subtract these 3- or 4-digit numbers.

1. 681
   + 145

2. 428
   − 119

3. 4,918
   + 3,928

4. 2,830
   − 519

5. 248
   + 48

6. 569
   − 247

7. 2,709
   + 1,282

8. 6,219
   − 4,356

9. 304
   − 172

10. 143
    + 219

11. 3,744
    − 1,378

12. 7,645
    − 564

Add the correct word—<u>their</u> or <u>there</u>. **<u>Remember</u>**: <u>their</u> means "they own" or "have," and <u>there</u> means "in or at the place," or it can begin a sentence.

1. _____ must be something wrong with that cow.

2. The Hills were training _____ horse to jump.

3. We are going to _____ farm tomorrow.

4. Please put the boxes over _____.

5. Will you please sit here, not _____?

6. _____ barn burned down yesterday.

Write four sentences about your school. Use <u>their</u> in two of them and <u>there</u> in the other two.

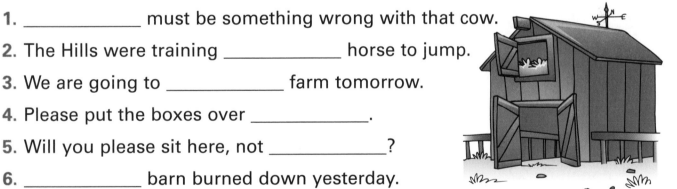

7. _____

8. _____

9. _____

10. _____

A <u>suffix</u> is a syllable added to the end of a base word.
Add the suffix in the middle of the suffix wheel to the end of the
base word. Write the new word. <u>Remember</u>: You may need to double
the final consonant or change a <u>y</u> to an <u>i</u> when adding a suffix.

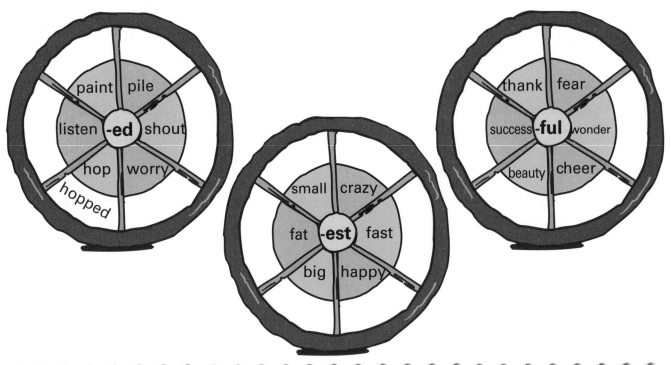

Producers and Consumers. Write answers to the following questions
or discuss them with an adult.

1. Name some producers. _____

2. How are producers and consumers different?_____

    _____

3. What do profit, labor, and wages have to do with producers and

    consumers? _____

4. How are producers and consumers interdependent? _____

    _____

5. How do you think consumers and producers of today are different from

    consumers and producers of years ago? _____

    _____

Give the integer for each letter on the number line.

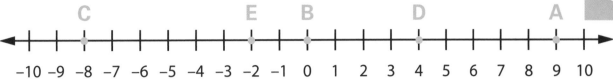

C   E   B   D   A

-10 -9 -8 -7 -6 -5 -4 -3 -2 -1 0 1 2 3 4 5 6 7 8 9 10

1. A = _____   **2.** B = _____   **3.** C = _____   **4.** D = _____   **5.** E = _____

Use <, >, or = for each ◯.

1. ⁻8 ◯ 8   **2.** 0 ◯ ⁻3

3. 15 ◯ ⁻16   **4.** |⁻4| ◯ 4

5. ⁻12 ◯ ⁻20   **6.** ⁻3 ◯ |⁻4|

Read the following paragraph and answer the questions.

Kangaroos are furry, hopping mammals that live only in Australia. Antelope kangaroos live on the plains in the north. Gray kangaroos live mostly in the grasslands and forests of eastern and southern Australia. Red kangaroos make their home in the deserts and dry grasslands in the central part of the country, and most wallaroos live in dry, rocky hills.

1. What is the main idea of this paragraph?

_____

_____

_____

2. List some of the important details of the paragraph.

_____

_____

_____

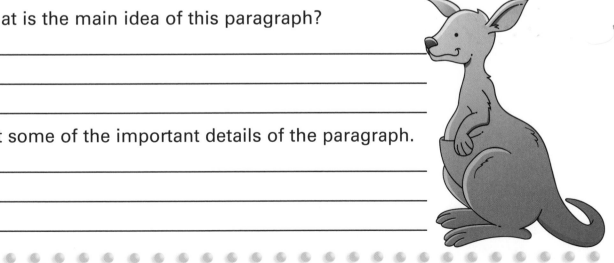

What products might we get from the <u>seven major regions</u> of our country? See if you can put the correct region next to the correct products.

- **Great Lakes**
- **Plains**
- **Mountain**
- **Pacific**
- **Southwest**
- **Southeast**
- **Northeast**

_____ 1. The main crops are sugarcane, oranges, soybeans, rice, peanuts, and tobacco. The main minerals are oil, iron ore, limestone, and coal. Hickory, oak, maple, and lots of other trees are used for furniture, paper, and other products.

_____ 2. Fish and shellfish are found here: cod, butterfish, clams, lobsters, squid, sea bass, flounder, sole, and swordfish. Farm products include milk, cheese, eggs, fruits, vegetables, chickens, turkeys, tomatoes, blueberries, cranberries, maple syrup, and grapes. This region also produces lots of coal.

_____ 3. Record amounts of corn, soybeans, and oats are found here. Other crops include fruits and vegetables. This area is rich in minerals, iron ore, and coal. This area is also rich in dairy products. This is called the "Corn Belt" of the United States.

_____ 4. Corn and wheat grow well here. A lot of farming, ranching, and mining is done here. Manufacturers produce hot dogs, flour, and breakfast cereals.

_____ 5. The largest crop in this area is cotton. Other crops are oranges, grapefruit, rice, and wheat. They raise lots of cattle and sheep here. Silver and copper are found in this region. Fuels are also plentiful, such as coal, natural gas, uranium, and oil.

_____ 6. A wide variety of products come from here because of the two very different climate areas. Products include oil, king crab, salmon, and timber, as well as pineapple, macadamia nuts, fruits, nuts, berries, and vegetables. This area also produces petroleum and natural gas. It has the <u>top</u> agricultural state in the nation, as well as the top commercial fishing region.

_____ 7. Some of the major minerals found in this region are gold, lead, silver, copper, and zinc. There is also lots of natural gas, coal, and oil to be found. Wheat, peas, beans, sugar beets, and potatoes are grown here. Ranching includes beef cattle, sheep, and dairy cows.

Estimating Sums and Differences. When estimating numbers, round them off; then add or subtract. <u>Remember</u>: Answers are not exact.

EXAMPLE: 420 + 384 = ___. 420 is close to <u>400</u>, and 384 is close to <u>400</u>, so your answer would be <u>800</u> when estimating. Try estimating these problems!

1. 88 + 19 = _____

2. 81 + 75 = _____

3. 93 – 85 = _____

4. 98 – 12 = _____

5. 93 – 39 = _____

6. 891 – 551 = _____

7. 57 – 39 = _____

8. 24 + 35 = _____

9. 209 + 179 = _____

10. 64 + 39 = _____

11. 56 – 33 = _____

12. 288 + 398 = _____

13. 66 + 12 = _____

14. 30 + 71 = _____

15. 610 – 273 = _____

Write the five steps to the writing or composition process. (See page 59 if you need help.) Then write a short story of your own. Use all five steps. You will need additional paper.

Story: _____

_____

_____

_____

_____

_____

_____

_____

_____

_____

_____

Prefixes are syllables added to the beginning of a base word. Add a prefix to these base words.

FACTOID
Every time you lick a stamp, you're consuming 1/10 of a calorie.

1. Will you **un** lock the door?

2. Can you ____call what he said?

3. The genie will ____appear if you clap your hands.

4. Janet will ____fold the napkins.

5. Do you ____agree with what I said?

6. Mother is going to ____arrange the front room.

7. The picture was the shape of a ____angle.

8. Everyone needs to come ____board now.

9. Erin and Eli will wear ____forms to the game.

10. You can count on me to ____pay you.

11. Look out for the ____coming traffic!

12. The Damons have six ____phones in their house.

A **metaphor** compares two different things.
Here are a few metaphors written by students:

Homework is a sweaty sock: it stinks!

People are mirrors; you can see yourself in them.

Sleep is a stone, quiet and still.

Write your own metaphors by comparing two different things.

1. Sleep is _____

2. Life is _____

3. Anger is_____

4. Happiness is_____

5. Friendship is_____

Number Families. You can practice basic math facts by using "families of facts."

7 + 2 = 9	2 + 7 = 9	9 − 2 = 7	9 − 7 = 2
3 x 6 = 18	6 x 3 = 18	18 ÷ 3 = 6	18 ÷ 6 = 3

Complete the number families below.

1. 9, 7, 16

  9 + 7 = 16

  ___ + ___ = ___

  ___ − ___ = ___

  ___ − ___ = ___

2. 3, 9, 27

  3 x 9 = 27

  ___ x ___ = ___

  ___ ÷ ___ = ___

  ___ ÷ ___ = ___

3. 8, 5, 40

  8 x 5 = 40

  ___ x ___ = ___

  ___ ÷ ___ = ___

  ___ ÷ ___ = ___

4. 3, 8, 11

  3 + 8 = 11

  ___ + ___ = ___

  ___ − ___ = ___

  ___ − ___ = ___

5. 3, 4, 12

  3 x 4 = 12

  ___ x ___ = ___

  ___ ÷ ___ = ___

  ___ ÷ ___ = ___

6. 612, 208, 820

  612 + 208 = 820

  ___ + ___ = ___

  ___ − ___ = ___

  ___ − ___ = ___

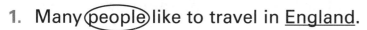

Nouns are words that name people, places, or things.
Common nouns name any person, place, or thing.
Proper nouns name a particular person, place, or thing.
Draw a (circle) around the common nouns and underline the proper nouns in the following sentences. The first one has been done for you.

1. Many (people) like to travel in England.
2. Christopher Columbus was an explorer.
3. Antarctica is a continent.
4. The ships crossed the Atlantic Ocean.
5. We paddled the canoe down the Red River.
6. Astronauts explore space for the United States.
7. San Francisco is the city by the bay.
8. Julie and Ashley visited their aunt in Boston.
9. Mt. Smart is a small mountain in Idaho.
10. Thursday is Andrew's birthday.

Draw lines between these words and their abbreviations.

EXAMPLE:

Sunday	mag.	Friday	tel.
magazine	pd.	principal	Fri.
quart	ex.	telephone	pt.
November	Sun.	volume	ave.
paid	oz.	pint	Oct.
pages	pkg.	William	wk.
ounce	Nov.	October	prin.
package	qt.	street	st.
government	pp.	avenue	Wm.
example	govt.	week	vol.

Our Government. There are three kinds of government: <u>local</u>, <u>state</u>, and <u>federal</u> (or national). Each kind handles problems of different sizes. They try to solve problems that people cannot solve alone. Put the following statements on problem solving and choices in the correct sequence (1, 2, 3, 4).

_____ Write down the possible results of each choice, whether good or bad.

_____ List all the choices or possibilities there are in connection to the problem or situation.

_____ If there is more than one person involved, or if it involves <u>money</u>, people take a vote.

_____ Decide what is most important and which choice or choices will best solve the problem.

Now choose a problem or choice that you are facing and try to follow some or all of the steps above. This problem or choice may affect just you, or it might affect those around you.

Money Sense. Make sense of these money problems.

1. Cammie has 3 coins worth 11¢. What are the coins?

   _____

   _____

2. Janet has 6 coins worth 47¢. What are the coins?

   _____

   _____

3. Frankie has 5 coins worth 17¢. What 5 coins add up to 17¢?

   _____

   _____

4. Tenley has 7 coins. The value of the coins is 20¢. Find 7 coins with the value of 20¢.

   _____

   _____

5. Jake has 4 coins. One of them is a quarter. The value of his coins is 45¢. What coins does he have?

   _____

   _____

6. Gary has 6 coins worth 40¢. Find the 6 coins that Gary has with the value of 40¢.

   _____

   _____

Singular (One) Nouns and Plural (More Than One) Nouns. Write the singular or plural form of the following nouns.

EXAMPLE:

bee _____*bees*_____

1. bunny _____
3. cities _____
5. toe _____
7. buses _____
9. branch _____
11. foot _____
13. sheep _____
15. men _____
17. face _____
19. berries _____

EXAMPLE:

boys _____*boy*_____

2. windows _____
4. child _____
6. libraries _____
8. movie _____
10. goose _____
12. deer _____
14. boxes _____
16. class _____
18. woman _____
20. tax _____

Which word referent should be used in place of the word or words in parenthesis? Write it in the blank. <u>He</u>, <u>she</u>, <u>you</u>, <u>it</u>, <u>they</u>, <u>him</u>, <u>her</u>, <u>them</u>, <u>then</u>, <u>here</u>, <u>us</u>, and <u>there</u> are all word referents.

Barbara and Denise were best friends. (Barbara and Denise) _____ had decided to go on a trip together this summer. With maps and brochures scattered all over Barbara's floor, (Barbara and Denise) _____ started looking for a place to go. One brochure described an interesting place. (The brochure) _____ was about Yellowstone Park. "Let's go (Yellowstone) _____!" cried Denise. "(Yellowstone) _____ would be a fun place to go. I think we should ask my brother to go with us," said Barbara. "(My brother) _____ could do a lot of the driving for (Barbara and Denise) _____."

Tom's car was packed and ready to go the next morning. (The car) _____ was a new 4x4 Ranger. (Barbara, Denise, and Tom) _____ would have taken Barbara's car, but (Barbara's) _____ car had a flat tire.

After driving for two days the travelers got to Yellowstone Park. Tom shouted, "At last we are (at Yellowstone) _____!" (Tom) _____ was tired of driving. (The trip) _____ turned out to be a fun trip for (Barbara, Denise, and Tom) _____.

• •

Points of Interest. What makes the town, state, or country that you live in an interesting place? Write an advertisement to get people to visit or even live in your town, state, or country. What are the points of interest? What makes it special and different from other places?

_____

_____

_____

_____

_____

_____

_____

Geometry Gems

Remember: <u>Parallel</u> <u>lines</u> never meet. <u>Perpendicular</u> <u>lines</u> form a right angle where they meet.

Draw a red line parallel to each line segment below.

1.

2.

3.

Draw a blue line perpendicular to each line segment below.

4.

5.

6.

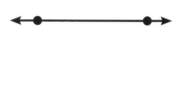

Write a proper noun for each of the common nouns listed below.
Remember: Proper nouns start with capital letters.

EXAMPLE:

1. building _White House_

2. person _____

3. holiday _____

4. desert _____

5. national park _____

6. day _____

7. state _____

8. island _____

9. river _____

10. street _____

Now write a common noun for the following proper nouns.

1. Golden Gate _____

2. Canada _____

3. San Francisco _____

4. Joseph _____

5. Pacific _____

6. Liberty Bell _____

7. November _____

8. Iroquois _____

Father's Day. Write about fathers; then draw a picture. Fathers should always… Fathers should never… If I were a father I would want to always…

FACTOID
Squirrels have helped many trees to grow by burying nuts and forgetting where they hid them.

_____

_____

_____

_____

_____

_____

_____

_____

_____

_____

_____

Draw your picture here!

_____

_____

_____

_____

_____

_____

_____

_____

_____

_____

_____

Adding Thousands. If you have a calculator, use it to check your answers.

1. 2,456
    + 1,527

2. 9,873
    + 1,828

3. 4,678
    + 3,321

4. 18,086
    + 12,302

5. 19,873
    + 1,828

6. 1,465
    + 3,035

7. 626
    8,024
    + 3,643

8. 3,481
    309
    + 4,877

9. 430
    2,824
    + 4,099

• •

A singular (one) possessive noun is usually formed by adding 's—animal's. A plural (two or more) possessive noun is usually formed by adding s'—animals'. Choose a singular or plural possessive noun from the Word Bank to fill in the blanks. <u>Hint</u>: Look at the word after the blank to help you decide if you need a singular or plural.

Word Bank
birds'
woman's
child's
dog's
children's
Rabbits'
cows'
lady's
plumbers'
Ann's

1. The _____ toy is broken.

2. _____ tails are fluffy.

3. My _____ leash is black.

4. After the accident the _____ tools were all over the road.

5. The _____ pets are in a pet show.

6. The _____ coat is made of fur.

7. We hope that _____ picture will win the prize.

8. The _____ mooing was loud and noisy.

9. That _____ hat blew away in the windstorm.

10. The _____ nests were high up in the trees.

Write the contractions to fill in the circles of the puzzle.

FACTOID
Pure gold is too soft to use in jewelry. Other metals are added to the gold to make it stronger.

1. I would   Ⓘ ' ⓓ
2. is not   ○ ○ ○ ' ○
3. they will   ○ ○ ○ ○ ' ○ ○
4. should have   ○ ○ ○ ○ ○ ' ○ ○
5. who are   ○ ○ ○ ' ○ ○
6. these will   ○ ○ ○ ○ ○ ' ○ ○
7. must not   ○ ○ ○ ○ ○ ' ○
8. there have   ○ ○ ○ ○ ○ ' ○ ○
9. need not   ○ ○ ○ ○ ○ ' ○
10. it had   ○ ○ ' ○
11. will not   ○ ○ ○ ' ○
12. what has   ○ ○ ○ ○ ' ○

Regions of Our Country. Our country is divided into seven regions. <u>Great Lakes</u>, <u>Plains</u>, <u>Mountain</u>, and <u>Pacific</u> are all regions named after bodies of water or important landforms. The other three major regions, <u>Southwest</u>, <u>Southeast</u>, and <u>Northeast</u>, are named for intermediate directions. Label the seven major regions of our United States.

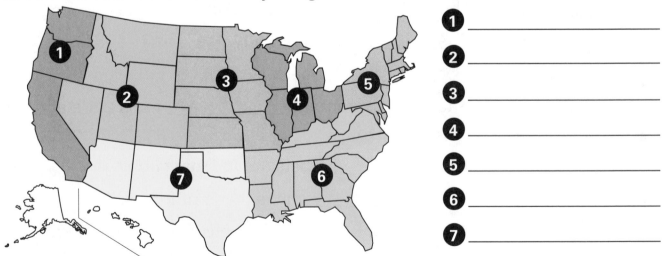

1. _____
2. _____
3. _____
4. _____
5. _____
6. _____
7. _____

*Something to think about. What about Hawaii and Alaska? What region or direction would they belong to?

Hawaii_____   Alaska_____

Subtracting Thousands. Check your answers with a calculator if you have one.

1. 4,888
    − 1,777

2. 4,314
    − 2,532

3. 3,826
    −   49

4. 5,835
    − 1,290

5. 2,182
    −   396

6. 6,922
    − 5,833

7. 2,493
    − 1,617

8. 22,318
    − 17,725

9. 57,260
    − 23,458

Write the singular and plural possessive forms of the following nouns. The first one is done for you.

Singular	Possessive	Plural	Possessive
boy	*boy's*	boys	*boys'*
key		keys	
bird		birds	
mouse		mice	
puppy		puppies	
woman		women	
class		classes	
rollerblade		rollerblades	
flag		flags	
computer		computers	

Cross out the word that does not belong in the sentence.

EXAMPLE: It's great that we ~~is~~ often agree on things.

1. All butterflies will be gone went by October.
2. Idaho are is known as the "Potato State."
3. She will hid hide behind that large old tree.
4. I have ridden rode my horse regularly this summer.
5. Our dog consistently goes to that corner to dig digging.
6. My baby sister always drinks dranks her milk.
7. Lee Ann had to swept sweep out the garage.
8. I were was very irritated with my friend.
9. How long have you known know Susan Green?
10. We have has been forbidden to go into the cave.
11. Have you done did your chores?
12. The scared boy ran run all the way home.

Time Zones. Unscramble the answers.

Pacific

Mountain

Central

Eastern

1. Time zones are different because of the usn. _____
2. As we go east the time is treal. _____
3. As we go west the time is rrilaee. _____
4. You can find time zone maps in a lwdro manaacl. _____
5. If you want to find the time in a certain zone to the east, you might want to dad suohr _____, not trtbuacs suohr. _____
6. Remember, different parts of the world receive sunlight at different times. That is why we have different meit sonze. _____

Multiplication. Find each product.

EXAMPLE:

1. 9 x 2 = 18
2. 1 x 9 = _____
3. 7 x 9 = _____
4. 8 x 4 = _____
5. 4 x 7 = _____
6. 9 x 9 = _____
7. 5 x 6 = _____
8. 8 x 3 = _____
9. 8 x 5 = _____
10. 7 x 3 = _____
11. 3 x 3 = _____
12. 3 x 4 = _____
13. 4 x 6 = _____
14. 6 x 3 = _____
15. 5 x 5 = _____
16. 9 x 5 = _____
17. 6 x 9 = _____
18. 8 x 7 = _____
19. 8 x 6 = _____
20. 6 x 6 = _____
21. 7 x 3 = _____
22. 5 x 7 = _____
23. 9 x 4 = _____
24. 8 x 8 = _____
25. 3 x 9 = _____
26. 7 x 7 = _____
27. 9 x 11 = _____
28. 7 x 6 = _____
29. 7 x 8 = _____
30. 9 x 10 = _____

Main Verbs and Helping Verbs. Helping verbs help the main verb. The main verb shows action. Underline the main verbs. Circle the helping verbs.

EXAMPLE:

1. It (has been) <u>raining</u> for five days.
2. Jack had finished his lessons before 10:00.
3. I have enjoyed the children this month.
4. We were cleaning the house for our friend.
5. The babies have been sleeping for two hours.

Main Verbs

Helping Verbs

Fill in the blank with a helping verb.

6. David _____ diving into the pond.

7. The pool _____ _____ used all summer.

8. I _____ _____ waiting for them to fix it.

9. They _____ _____ working on it for three weeks.

10. It _____ _____ fun without the pool.

Calendar. The months of the year and the days of the week are written below in order. On the lines below write the months and days in alphabetical order. Write in cursive.

January February March April May June July
August September October November December
Sunday Monday Tuesday Wednesday Thursday Friday Saturday

1. _____

2. _____

3. _____

4. _____

5. _____

6. _____

7. _____

8. _____

9. _____

10. _____

11. _____

12. _____

13. _____

14. _____

15. _____

16. _____

17. _____

18. _____

19. _____

World Globe. Read the information given; then label the following:

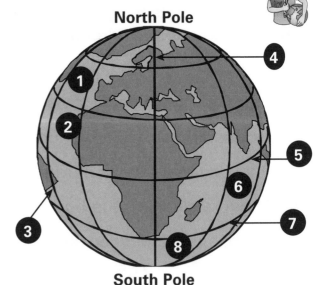

1. Northern _____
2. Western _____
3. Line of _____
4. Prime _____
5. _____
6. Eastern _____
7. Line of _____
8. Southern _____

We use different terms to locate places on maps and globes. We use lines of <u>latitude</u> to go around the globe from east to west. These lines run parallel to each other, never touching each other. Lines of <u>longitude</u> run north and south on a map or globe and are sometimes called <u>meridians</u>.

The <u>equator</u> is a line of <u>latitude</u> running west to east that divides the earth in half. The top half is called the <u>Northern Hemisphere</u>; the bottom half is called the <u>Southern Hemisphere</u>. The <u>prime meridian</u> is a line of <u>longitude</u>. It runs from north to south. All longitudes are determined based on the prime meridian.

Adding or Subtracting Thousands.
Check your answers using a calculator
if you have one.

1. 7,458
    − 3,762

2. 8,562
    + 2,163

3. 5,585
    − 2,609

4. 6,052
    − 5,381

5. 36,814
    − 7,523

6. 53,397
    + 39,288

7. 19,506
    + 34,947

8. 18,103
    − 9,079

9. 3,245
    5,029
    + 6,981

10. 9,421
    8,389
    + 4,506

11. 3,340
    7,189
    + 4,482

12. 46,306
    18,782
    + 3,115

Present tense verbs happen now. **Past tense** verbs have already happened. Write the past or present tense for these verbs.

	Present	Past		Present	Past
EX.	stay	*stayed*	1.	_____	thanked
2.	hop	_____	3.	_____	called
4.	skate	_____	5.	_____	sprained
6.	love	_____	7.	_____	wrapped
8.	play	_____	9.	_____	hugged

Past Tense with a Helper. Write the past tense.

	Present	Past Tense with Helping Verb
EX.	walk	has, have, had *walked*
1.	jog	has, have, had _____
2.	hurry	has, have, had _____
3.	empty	has, have, had _____
4.	chase	has, have, had _____

The Continental Congress adopted the first official American flag in Philadelphia, Pennsylvania, on June 14, 1777. History tells us that at that particular time the thirteen colonies were fighting for their liberty. The flag was a symbol of unity.
Choose one or more of the following activities.

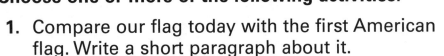

1. Compare our flag today with the first American flag. Write a short paragraph about it.
2. Write what your life may have been like during that time.
3. Find out what the stars, stripes, and colors of the flag stand for and write about them.

_____

_____

_____

_____

_____

_____

_____

Your Choice of Rooms. Choose a room in your house and measure the floor space. Measure it in either feet or meters. Draw and label it.

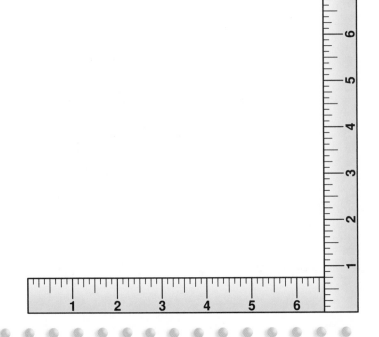

Division. Find each quotient.

1. $20 \div 4 =$ _____
2. $28 \div 4 =$ _____
3. $14 \div 7 =$ _____
4. $0 \div 2 =$ _____
5. $42 \div 6 =$ _____
6. $30 \div 5 =$ _____
7. $32 \div 4 =$ _____
8. $25 \div 5 =$ _____
9. $81 \div 9 =$ _____
10. $49 \div 7 =$ _____
11. $18 \div 6 =$ _____
12. $63 \div 7 =$ _____
13. $40 \div 5 =$ _____
14. $36 \div 9 =$ _____
15. $72 \div 9 =$ _____
16. $54 \div 6 =$ _____
17. $48 \div 6 =$ _____
18. $32 \div 8 =$ _____
19. $45 \div 9 =$ _____
20. $36 \div 6 =$ _____
21. $54 \div 9 =$ _____

Fill in the blanks with the past tense verb. <u>Hint:</u> You will have to change the spelling. The first one is done for you.

Present	Past Tense
EX. Bells <u>ring</u>.	Bells __*rang*__ .
1. We <u>eat</u>.	We _____ .
2. I <u>wear</u> it.	I _____ it.
3. I <u>throw</u> rocks.	I _____ rocks.
4. I <u>say</u> no.	I _____ no.
5. They <u>take</u> turns.	They _____ turns.

Fill in the blank with the past tense of the verb.

6. Sam _____ he wanted to stay in touch with Kit.   (know)
7. Katie _____ a letter to Ron.   (write)
8. He _____ his friend with him.   (bring)
9. The men _____ to dig the ditch.   (begin)
10. That little girl _____ her doll again.   (break)
11. I _____ her new car to the play.   (drive)

Replace the word <u>said</u> in these sentences with another word that fits the meaning.

EXAMPLE:

1. The man (said) _yelled_, "Get that cat out of here!"

2. Margaret (said) _____, "Please, don't do that."

3. Mother always (said) _____, "A stitch in time saves nine."

4. "Is it time to go home so soon?" (said) _____ Mike.

5. "I don't like vegetables in soups," (said) _____ Dad.

6. "My sore throat still hurts," (said) _____ Nicholas.

7. The boy with a mouth full of candy (said) _____ he wanted more.

8. I called Megan on the phone, and she (said) _____, "There's no school today."

9. The shopkeeper (said) _____, "Do you want red or orange socks?"

10. Kristine Jones (said) _____ her mother makes the best cookies.

Using Guide Words. Look at the words in the Word Bank. Print each word in alphabetical order below the two guide words it would appear between in a dictionary.

Word Bank	aggravate	aboard	about	aid	ailment
	above	affect	after	agree	afford

1. **aardvark**   **afghan**

_____

_____

_____

_____

2. **Africa**   **aim**

_____

_____

_____

_____

Multiplication with Three Factors. Find the product of the three factors.

EXAMPLE: 6 x 1 x 3 = **6 x 1 = 6 x 3 = 18**

1. 2 x 4 x 2 = ____   2. 3 x 3 x 5 = ____   3. 4 x 2 x 2 = ____   4. 2 x 5 x 1 = ____

5. 4 x 2 x 4 = ____   6. 2 x 3 x 7 = ____   7. 0 x 9 x 9 = ____   8. 3 x 2 x 3 = ____

9. 3 x 3 x 3 = ____   10. 5 x 2 x 2 = ____   11. 4 x 2 x 5 = ____   12. 2 x 3 x 6 = ____

13. 1 x 2 x 3 = ____   14. 3 x 3 x 0 = ____   15. 3 x 5 x 0 = ____   16. 1 x 3 x 5 = ____

17. 2 x 3 x 4 = ____   18. 2 x 2 x 3 = ____   19. 4 x 3 x 2 = ____   20. 8 x 1 x 8 = ____

Write two sentences using the word <u>our</u>. Write two sentences using the word <u>are</u>.

EX.
<u>Our</u> house is almost finished.

When <u>are</u> you going to live in it?

1. _____

2. _____

3. _____

4. _____

Now write two sentences using <u>it's</u> and two sentences using <u>its</u>.
Remember: <u>It's</u> is a contraction of <u>it is</u>, and <u>its</u> is a possessive pronoun.

1. _____

2. _____

3. _____

4. _____

A Trip to Outer Space. We're planning a big trip into outer space! You are invited to come along, too. You can even invite a few friends. What will you pack? Why? Where shall we go? What needs to be done? What do you think will happen? What will it be like? Think, then write!

FACTOID

Penguins have a special organ near their eyes that can change salt water into fresh water.

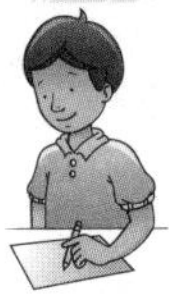

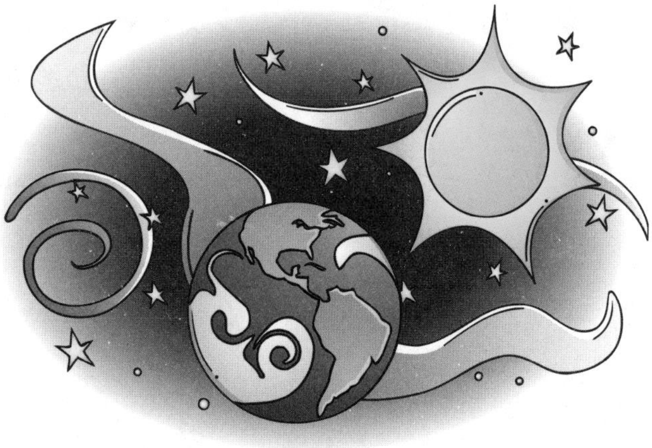

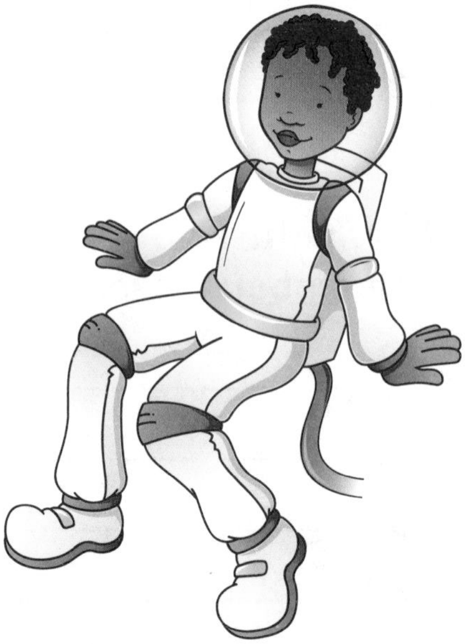

Problem Solving.

1. Jennifer bought a package of candy for $2.50. The tax was 19¢. She used a coupon for 42¢ off the price of the candy. How much did she pay? _____

2. Elsie worked at a grocery store keeping the shelves full. She worked 4 hours on Wednesday and 5 hours on Friday. She earned $5 an hour. How much did she earn that week? _____

3. Randy bought a box of cookies for $1.98. He used a 20¢ coupon. On this particular day, the store took off double the coupon's

value. How much did Randy pay for that box of cookies? _____

4. Bradley bought a shirt for $5 off the original price of $24. The tax was $1.40. How much did Bradley pay? _____

5. Gayle bought a 6-pack of canned orange juice for $2.89. The store had a special for 74¢ off the original price. The tax was 60¢. How much did Gayle spend? _____

• •

Match the word to the meaning. Use a dictionary.

EXAMPLE:

1. honorable   a kind of light

2. current   to make clearly known

3. knowledge   good reputation

4. suspicion   usual, familiar, common

5. exact   very large, great

6. lantern   occupation, source of livelihood

7. profession   leaving no room for error

8. universal   now in progress

9. agriculture   information, awareness, understanding

10. declare   understood by all

11. ordinary   the science and art of farming

12. tremendous   suspecting or being suspected

• •

Read the meanings below and see if you know what the words mean. Write the word by its meaning.

gnaw doubt scene glisten plain

pause pedal gnat comfort admire

1. to have high regard for; with wonder and delight   _____

2. a lever worked with the foot   _____

3. shine or sparkle   _____

4. to not believe; to feel unsure   _____

5. a short stop or wait   _____

6. freedom from hardship; to ease   _____

7. flatland; not fancy   _____

8. part of a play; show strong feelings in front of others _____

9. to bite at something or wear away   _____

10. small fly or insect   _____

Continents. Have you ever really looked at the shapes of the continents on a world map? It almost seems as if the continents are part of a big puzzle. Find a world map; then trace and cut out the following major continents and islands: North and South America, Australia, Europe–Asia, Greenland, and Africa. Try to fit all of the continents together so that no (or very little) space exists between them.

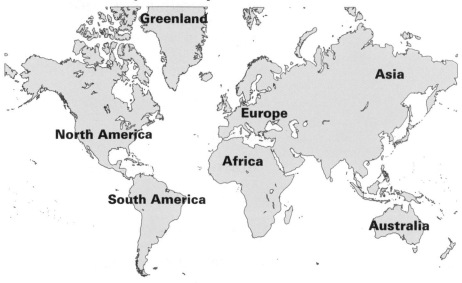

Divide to find the quotient.

1. $4\overline{)28}$ 2. $5\overline{)40}$ 3. $7\overline{)49}$ 4. $6\overline{)30}$

5. $8\overline{)72}$ 6. $9\overline{)45}$ 7. $8\overline{)32}$ 8. $3\overline{)15}$

9. $7\overline{)56}$ 10. $6\overline{)24}$ 11. $7\overline{)14}$ 12. $6\overline{)54}$

13. $9\overline{)9}$ 14. $7\overline{)28}$ 15. $6\overline{)42}$ 16. $8\overline{)56}$

17. $7\overline{)35}$ 18. $6\overline{)48}$ 19. $9\overline{)81}$ 20. $8\overline{)24}$

You have been out of school for a few weeks now. Write a story telling what you have been doing for the past few weeks. Be sure to follow the five steps of the writing process.

_____

_____

_____

_____

_____

_____

_____

_____

_____

_____

Below are the days of the week and the months of the year spelled with dictionary symbols. Write the words to the side. Don't forget capital letters.

1. /ā´pr əl/   *April*

2. /märch/ _____

3. /jan´ū er´ē/ _____

4. /wenz´dā/ _____

5. /mun´dā/ _____

6. /jün/ _____

7. /sep tem´b ər/ _____

8. /sun´dā/ _____

9. /dē sem´b ər/ _____

10. /nō vem´b ər/ _____

11. /sat´ ər dā/ _____

12. /o´gest/ _____

13. /mā/ _____

14. /th ər z´dā/ _____

15. /feb´rüer´ē/ _____

16. /ok tō b ər/ _____

17. /tūz´dā/ _____

18. /jülī´/ _____

19. /frī´dā/ _____

Chord—a line segment passing through a circle that has its endpoints on that circle

Circumference—the distance around a circle

Diameter—a chord passing through the center of a circle

Radius—a line segment with one endpoint at the center of a circle and the other endpoint on the circle

Draw an example for each term.

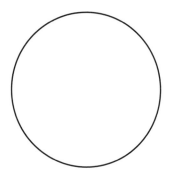

Draw a radius AB.

Draw a diameter XY.

Trace the circumference.

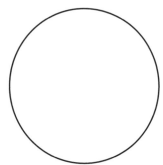

Draw a chord DE.

Eggs-traordinary!

This air pressure experiment can be an interesting way to eat breakfast, if your mom's not picky about you playing with your food!

Stuff You Need:
adult
egg (hard-boiled)
jar (small-mouth, like an olive jar)
matches (wooden)

Parent Alert: This experiment uses matches.
Make sure you supervise your child during this experiment!

Here's What to Do:

1. Peel a hard-boiled egg and place it on top of a clean, empty olive jar. Without breaking the egg, try your best to squish it into the jar. Bet you can't get it in there! It won't go in because the jar is full of air, which takes up space and doesn't like getting squished. So, it squishes back.

2. Take the egg off the jar. Stick three wooden matches in one end of the egg.

Always have adult supervision and watch what you're doing when using matches!
Be careful when lighting the matches and when turning the egg upside down on the jar.

3. Light the matches. Quickly place the egg on the bottle. Be sure the matches are inside the bottle, or this experiment won't work. Observe the reaction. Gulp! This is one hungry jar!

4. You now have a different problem. How do you get the egg OUT of the jar? Take a deep breath, tip the jar up so that the egg rests against the mouth of the jar, and blow quickly into the jar. The musty, old, smells-like-burned-paper egg will pop into your mouth. Fun, huh? And it tastes really good, too.

What's This All About?

The egg got into the jar because of air pressure. The heat from the burning matches increased the air pressure inside the jar, but the flame also removed oxygen from the air inside the jar, reducing the air pressure inside. When the flame went out, you were left with fewer air molecules and a lower air pressure inside the jar. The higher air pressure outside the jar then pushed the egg in.

You can get the egg out of the jar because when you blow into the jar, the burst of air increases the air pressure. The difference in air pressure pushes the egg back out of the opening. You might be able to do this experiment a couple of times, but the egg tends to fall apart from all this pushing and pulling.

Metamorphic Madness

Did you know that rocks can be cemented together with other rocks by heat and pressure to make bigger rocks? It is hard to recreate the pressure, but the heat makes this activity a good demonstration.

Stuff You Need:

adult
goggles
pebbles
stove top
metal food can (like a coffee can)

crayon pieces
hot pad (oven mitt)
sand
water

cupcake baking cup (paper)
paper (scraps)
saucepan

Parent Alert: This activity involves using a stove and hot wax. Use extreme caution! Wear goggles and be careful using the stove. Wax can burn, so don't use too much heat.

Here's What to Do:

1. Place the can in the saucepan. Add water to the saucepan so that it covers about half of the can. Place the saucepan on the stove top on medium heat.

2. As the water heats up, add crayon pieces to the can.

3. The crayons will melt and form a brown muck on the bottom of the can. Add the sand, paper scraps, and pebbles to create your "rock."

Use a hot pad (oven mitt) to lift the can.

4. When all of the crayons have melted, carefully pour the can's contents into the paper baking cup.

5. When the "rock" has cooled, pull the paper baking cup away.

This is similar to what happens when metamorphic rocks are made. Separate materials fuse together under high pressure and temperatures to form a rock.

What's This All About?

Some rocks are made from other rocks that have stuck together over time. These are called **metamorphic** rocks, and they are made when different rocks are pressed together by extreme pressure or very high temperatures.

Metamorphic means "changed in shape or form." One good example of a metamorphic rock is quartzite. This rock starts out as sediment that got smooshed into a rock called sandstone. As other rocks pile up on top of the layers of sandstone and it is heated by the interior of the earth, it gets cooked into a harder rock that we call quartzite. Another example is marble, which is just limestone that has been changed into a harder rock by heat and pressure. In this experiment, everything started out as separate pieces and fused (or grew together) into one big mass. The hot water melted the crayon, and everything mixed together.

Summer Bridge Activities™

Motivational Calendar

Month _____

My parents and I decided that if I complete
20 days of **Summer Bridge Activities**™ and
read _____ minutes a day, my incentive/reward will be:

_____

Child's Signature _____ Parent's Signature_____

Day 1	☆	📖	_____	Day 11	☆	📖	_____
Day 2	☆	📖	_____	Day 12	☆	📖	_____
Day 3	☆	📖	_____	Day 13	☆	📖	_____
Day 4	☆	📖	_____	Day 14	☆	📖	_____
Day 5	☆	📖	_____	Day 15	☆	📖	_____
Day 6	☆	📖	_____	Day 16	☆	📖	_____
Day 7	☆	📖	_____	Day 17	☆	📖	_____
Day 8	☆	📖	_____	Day 18	☆	📖	_____
Day 9	☆	📖	_____	Day 19	☆	📖	_____
Day 10	☆	📖	_____	Day 20	☆	📖	_____

Child: Color the ☆ for daily activities completed.
Color the 📖 for daily reading completed.

Parent: Initial the _____ when all activities are complete.

Discover Something New!

Fun Activity Ideas to Go Along with Section Two!

1. Give your dog a bath or ask your neighbor or friend if you can give his or her dog a bath.

2. Pack a lunch and go to the park.

3. Roast marshmallows over a fire or BBQ.

4. Draw the shape of your state and put a star where you live. Draw your state flower, motto, and bird.

5. Write a poem that rhymes.

6. Make a batch of cookies and take them to a sick friend, neighbor, or relative.

7. Plant some flower or vegetable seeds in a pot and watch them grow.

8. Organize an earthquake drill for your family.

9. Get a piece of paper that is as long and as wide as you. Lie down on it and have someone outline you with a marker. Then color in the details—eyes, ears, mouth, clothes, arms, hands, etc.

10. Make a "Happy Birthday" card for a friend who is celebrating a birthday and give it to that person on his or her special day.

11. With bright colored markers, draw a picture of your favorite place to go. Paste it to a piece of posterboard and cut it into pieces for a jigsaw puzzle.

12. Make and fly a kite.

13. Invite your friends over for popcorn and vote on your favorite Disney movie. Watch the winning movie; then choose parts and act out the movie in your own way.

14. Read to younger children in your family or neighborhood.

15. Visit the library and attend story time.

16. Pick one of your favorite foods and learn how to make it.

17. Prepare a clean bed for your pet.

18. Get your neighborhood friends together and make a card of appreciation for the fire station closest to you. Then all of you deliver the card and take a tour of the station.

19. Invent a new game and play it with your friends.

20. Surprise a family member with breakfast in bed.

Write the rest of the number families.

1. 6 x 9 = 54 **9 x 6 = 54** **54 ÷ 6 = 9** **54 ÷ 9 = 6**	2. 8 x 7 = 56	3. 6 x 7 = 42
4. 48 ÷ 6 = 8	5. 72 ÷ 8 = 9	6. 6 x 9 = 54
7. 36 ÷ 4 = 9	8. 9 x 7 = 63	9. 5 x 9 = 45

Prefixes and Suffixes. <u>Remember</u>: Prefixes are added to the beginning of a base word. Suffixes are added to the end of a base word. Add a prefix to these words. Use <u>mis-</u>, <u>un-</u>, and <u>re-</u>. Write the whole word.

1. lucky _____	2. judge _____
3. spell _____	4. fill _____
5. build _____	6. able _____

Add a suffix to these words. Use <u>-er</u>, <u>-less</u>, <u>-ful</u>, and <u>-ed</u>. Write the whole word.

7. use _____	8. spell _____
9. care _____	10. hope _____
11. sing _____	12. teach _____

Now write two sentences using words of your choice from each of the two word lists above.

1. _____

2. _____

Opinions. Everyone has opinions on most things that happen around them. People will listen to your opinion more often if you state clearly and plainly why you feel as you do.

Write your opinion on one of the following topics or choose one of your own to write about.

1. People should always wear seat belts.
2. Children should be able to eat anything they want.
3. Schoolchildren should never have homework to do.
4. We should always help other people, whether they are in our country or not.

_____

_____

_____

_____

_____

_____

_____

_____

_____

_____

_____

_____

_____

_____

_____

_____

_____

I think kids should be able to choose their OWN bedtimes!

Find the product by multiplying.

EXAMPLE:
1
12
x 6
72

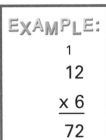

1. 12
   x 4

2. 22
   x 6

3. 18
   x 2

4. 23
   x 4

5. 23
   x 7

6. 34
   x 6

7. 16
   x 5

8. 78
   x 5

9. 86
   x 7

10. 69
   x 9

11. 57
   x 4

12. 62
   x 6

13. 97
   x 7

Think of your five senses to help you describe the words below. Try to come up with a word for each sense.

EXAMPLE:	taste	touch	smell	sight	sound
fire	smoky	hot	smoky	bright	crackle
candy bar	sweet	smooth	chocolate	brown	crunchy

1. a red rose _____

2. a rainbow _____

3. a barnyard _____

4. a snake's skin _____

5. a snowflake _____

Choose one of the above and write a paragraph about it. Be very descriptive and put in a lot of details.

_____

_____

_____

_____

Prefixes and suffixes can be added to word parts as well as to base or root words. Add a prefix or suffix to these word parts; then find and fill in the word shapes below.

1. _du_ plex

2. pott __ __ __

3. __ __ __ dora

4. __ __ most

5. __ __ mit

6. __ __ __ gress

7. gran __ __ __

8. fur __ __ __ __

9. don __ __

10. __ __ __ tant

11. __ __ plicate

12. __ __ do

[word shapes]

d|u|p|l|e|x

● ●

Mystery Word. Read the following clues to discover the mystery word.

1. It's composed of mineral particles mixed with animal and plant matter.

2. A well-organized, complicated layer of debris covering most of the earth's land surface.

3. It is shallow in some places and deep in other places.

4. It can be very red or very black, as well as other shades and colors.

5. It is one of the most important natural resources of any country.

6. It is so important that we need to make great efforts to conserve it.

7. It takes a long time to form.

8. A geologist thinks of it as material that covers the solid rock below the earth's surface.

9. To the farmer and most other people, it is a thin layer of the earth's surface that supports the growth of all kinds of plants.

10. The engineer thinks of it as material on which to build buildings, roads, earth dams, and landing strips.

Complete the tables.

1. There are 5 pennies in a nickel.

pennies	5	10	15	20	25	30
nickels	1					

2. There are 10 dimes in a dollar.

dimes	10	20	30			
dollars	1	2				

3. There are 6 cans of pop in each carton.

cans	6	12		24		
cartons	1		3		5	36

When you write something, your reader should be able to understand clearly what you are trying to say. Read the sentences below and change the underlined word to a more descriptive or exact word.

EXAMPLE:

This is a good book. _awesome_

1. My teacher is nice. _____

2. Your things will be safe here. _____

3. That is a big building. _____

4. A car went by our house. _____

5. Our pictures of the trip turned out badly. _____

6. This is a good sandwich. _____

7. The little boy saw a pretty butterfly. _____

8. Many big worms were crawling on the ground. _____

9. We had a bad winter. _____

10. These grapes are awful. _____

Most words spelled backwards don't mean anything, but some do. Here are clues for some words that become different words when they are written backwards. The first one is done for you.

1. Spell a word backwards for something you cook in, and you will have a word that means "siesta." *pan* & *nap*

2. Spell a word backwards for a name, and you will have something you turn on to get water. _____ & _____

3. Spell a word backwards for something you catch a fish in, and you will have a number. _____ & _____

4. Spell a word backwards for something to carry things in, and you will get a word that tells what you like to do with your friends. _____ & _____

5. Spell a word backwards for something a train needs, and you will get a word for someone who is not honest. _____ & _____

6. Spell a word for "victory" backwards, and you will have a word that means "at once." _____ & _____

7. Spell a word backwards for something to catch a mouse in, and you will get a word that means "something less than whole." _____ & _____

8. Spell a word backwards for a tool that cuts wood, and you will get a word that is a verb. _____ & _____

9. Spell a word backwards for a flying mammal, and you will get a word that means "a bill or check." _____ & _____

10. Spell a word backwards for the end of your pen, and you will have a word that means "a hole in the ground." _____ & _____

11. Spell a word backwards that means something you bathe in, and you will have a word that means "other than." _____ & _____

12. Spell a word backwards for "an instrument used in doing work," and you will get a word that means "things taken in a robbery." _____ & _____

Your little finger is about 1 centimeter wide. If you don't have a centimeter tape, use a string and this centimeter ruler to measure for the following activities.

cm 1 2 3 4 5 6 7 8 9 10 11 12 13 14 15

1. The length of your shoes _____

2. The length and width of this book _____, _____

3. Your neck measurement _____

4. Your kitchen table length and width _____, _____

5. Your height in centimeters _____

6. The width of a chair in your home _____

How many other things can you measure? Try estimating; then check to see how close you come to the exact measurement.

_____

_____

_____

_____

_____

Underline the pronouns in the following sentences.
Remember: A pronoun takes the place of a noun.

1. Will you go with us?

2. Tomorrow we will go home.

3. He did a good job.

4. This book came for him.

5. She went with me.

6. A package came for us.

7. We ate all of them.

8. You are a good sport.

9. It is time for her to go.

10. He and I ate the apples.

11. I thanked him for it.

12. It was very good.

Personification is when a writer gives human qualities to a non-living thing. An example of this is when the flower in *Alice in Wonderland* talks to Alice. Personify (or give life to) the following things by creating a conversation between them.

What would a

1. pencil say to a hand?_____
_____

2. carpet say to a foot? _____
_____

3. basketball say to a basketball player? _____
_____

4. skateboard say to a skateboarder? _____
_____

Bugs, Bugs, and More Bugs. The world has so many different kinds of bugs, but there's always room for one more. Create a brand new type of bug. Describe it. Where does it live? What does it do? What does it eat? How does it survive? Who are its friends or enemies?

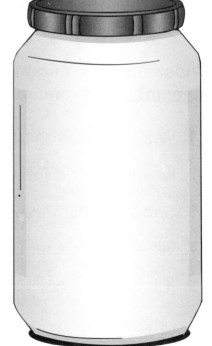

_____
_____
_____
_____
_____
_____
_____
_____
_____
_____
_____

Multiplying with tens and hundreds is fast and fun.

1. 4 x 10 = _____
2. 600 x 6 = _____
3. 7 x 800 = _____
4. 30 x 8 = _____
5. 5 x 20 = _____
6. 800 x 5 = _____
7. 8 x 90 = _____
8. 50 x 6 = _____
9. 600 x 5 = _____
10. 4 x 100 = _____
11. 7 x 80 = _____
12. 7 x 500 = _____
13. 900 x 7 = _____
14. 600 x 4 = _____
15. 900 x 4 = _____
16. 8 x 900 = _____
17. 800 x 2 = _____
18. 7 x 900 = _____
19. 3 x 10 = _____
20. 700 x 6 = _____
21. 3 x 800 = _____
22. 7 x 40 = _____
23. 9 x 10 = _____
24. 10 x 100 = _____
25. 4 x 60 = _____
26. 80 x 2 = _____
27. 500 x 4 = _____
28. 7 x 700 = _____
29. 30 x 8 = _____
30. 800 x 6 = _____

Pronouns such as <u>I</u>, <u>you</u>, <u>he</u>, <u>she</u>, <u>it</u>, <u>we</u>, and <u>they</u> can be the subject of a sentence. Read these sentences. The subject is underlined. Rewrite the sentences and use a subject pronoun in place of the underlined subject. Write in cursive.

1. <u>Jim and I</u> went fishing with our dad.

_____

2. <u>The weather</u> was sunny and warm.

_____

3. <u>Ann and Sue</u> can help us with the bait.

_____

4. <u>Mr. Jack</u> broke his leg.

_____

5. <u>Kathy</u> is going to New York on a vacation.

_____

Categorize these words under one of the headings.
Hint: There can be eight words under each heading.
Remember: Categorizing words means to put them in groups that have something in common. One row of examples is given.

~~interstate~~	~~add~~	~~region~~	~~colony~~	~~bacteria~~	solid
oxygen	city	hemisphere	stop	column	inch
debate	larva	yield	basin	hexagon	canal
environment	speed	equal	fossil	candidate	intersection
measure	insect	bay	caution	map	estimate
numerator	freedom	society	elevation	freeway	railroad

__Math Words__	__Geography Words__	__Transportation Words__	__Science Words__	__Social Studies Words__
add	*region*	*interstate*	*bacteria*	*colony*

What About These Animals in Our Country? Buffalo, condors, and grizzly bears have all but disappeared from our country. The symbol of our country, the bald eagle, is very rare in most states. Bald eagles and bears live in mountainous regions. Prairie dogs and antelope live on the plains. Alligators live in marshy areas. Rattlesnakes live in the desert. Wild turkeys can be found in wilderness areas. There are also many others. Choose one of the following to do on a separate piece of paper.

1. Draw a picture of an animal from our country. Place it in the correct habitat. Color it accurately. What other interesting animals do you think might belong in this area? Draw them. What other important information does your picture show?

2. If you choose not to draw a picture about an animal, write a paragraph about one. Use the same type of information that the picture would portray.

What animal(s) did you choose? _____

_____

_____

Addition and multiplication are related. Answer the addition problems and then write the related multiplication problem.

EXAMPLE: **10 + 10 + 10 + 10 + 10 = 50, or 5 x 10 = 50**

1. 20 + 20 + 20 = _____   _____ x _____ = _____

2. 9 + 9 + 9 + 9 + 9 + 9 = _____   _____ x _____ = _____

3. 100 + 100 + 100 + 100 = _____   _____ x _____ = _____

4. 8 + 8 + 8 + 8 + 8 + 8 + 8 + 8 = _____   _____ x _____ = _____

5. 12 + 12 + 12 + 12 = _____   _____ x _____ = _____

6. 75 + 75 + 75 = _____   _____ x _____ = _____

7. 35 + 35 + 35 + 35 + 35 + 35 = _____   _____ x _____ = _____

8. 51 + 51 + 51 + 51 + 51 = _____   _____ x _____ = _____

Use the pronouns me, her, him, it, us, you, and them after action verbs. Use I and me after the other nouns or pronouns. Circle the correct pronoun in each sentence.

1. Lily and (I, me) like to visit museums.

2. (They, Them) were very juicy oranges.

3. He helped her and (I, me).

4. (We, Us) tried not to fall as much this time.

5. Miss Green gave a shovel and bucket to (he, him).

6. (I, Me) wanted a new horse for Christmas.

7. Rick asked (she, her) to come with us.

8. Jason went with (they, them) to the mountain.

9. Mother asked (I, me) to fix the dinner.

10. Carla got some forks for (we, us).

me   her   him   it   us   them   you

Study this table about trees, and use it to answer the questions below. Can you identify the trees around you?

Tree	Bark	Wood	Leaves
Elm	brown and rough	strong	oval-shaped, saw-toothed edges, sharp points
Birch	creamy white, peels off in layers	elastic, won't break easily	heart-shaped or triangular with pointed tips
Oak	dark gray, thick, rough, deeply furrowed	hard, fine-grained	round, finger-shaped lobes
Willow	rough and broken	brown, soft, light	long, narrow, curved at tips
Maple	rough gray	strong	grow in pairs and are shaped like your open hand
Hickory	loose, peels off	white, hard	shaped like spearheads
Christmas Holly	ash colored	hard and fine-grained	glossy, sharp-pointed

1. Which tree has heart-shaped leaves? _____
   Hand-shaped? _____

2. How many trees have hard wood? _____

3. Which trees have sharp-pointed leaves? _____

4. Which tree has wood like a rubber band? _____

5. How many different colors of bark does the table show? _____
   Name them: _____

6. Which tree do you think we get syrup from? _____

7. Which tree bark do you think Indians used to cover their canoes? _____

8. Look around your yard and neighborhood. Can you identify any of the trees from the table? If so, which ones? _____

Complete this multiplication table.

x	10	20	30	40	50	60	70	80	90
1	10	20					70		
2						120			
3		60							270
4				160					
5							350		
6									
7		210							
8						480			
9				360					

How does multiplying by hundreds differ from multiplying by tens?

_____

Could you change this table to show multiplying by hundreds? _____

How? _____

Using Its, It's, Your, and You're. It's and you're are contractions. Its and your are possessive pronouns. Fill in the blanks with it's, its, your, or you're.

1. I hope _____ coming to my barn dance.

2. The dance will be for _____ friends also.

3. Do you think _____ too cold for a barn dance?

4. _____ starting time is eight o'clock.

5. Will _____ family come to the dance with you?

6. _____ floor is long and wide.

7. _____ coming early, aren't you?

8. I think I will need _____ help.

Write a sentence of your own for each word.

9. it's _____

10. its _____

11. you're _____

12. your _____

it's
its
you're
your

Read this crazy story. Every time you come to an underlined word, write the abbreviation for it. The first one is done for you.

Last January _Jan._ we moved from Georgia _____ to New York _____. It was a very long trip. We had to walk most of the way because the car broke down. We left on Monday _____, March _____ 10, and didn't get there until five years _____ later.

On the trip I had to learn how to measure. One day I measured gallons _____, inches, _____, yards _____, and grams _____. I also learned about science _____, adverbs _____, and adjectives _____. It was a boring trip!

We only traveled about two miles per hour _____. That's why it took us so long. Also, we stopped at a number _____ of relatives' places and stayed for months _____ on end.

Next time let's fly!

● ●

Table of Contents.

1. On what page of the guide would you find what kind of fast-food places are in town?

   _____

2. On what page would there be information about what the weather is like? _____

3. You want to see if any good movies are playing; what page would you look under? _____

4. You want to see if there are any job openings; what page would you look under? _____

5. You want a copy of the bus schedule; what page would you find it on? _____

Corvallis Happenings Guide:
Local Information,
Table of Contents

What About Time? You know that 60 seconds = 1 minute, 60 minutes = 1 hour, 24 hours = 1 day, 7 days = 1 week, 52 weeks = 1 year, 12 months = 1 year, and 365 days = 1 year (except leap year, which has 366 days).

Use what you know to complete the following.

1. Phillip is in the fourth grade. He is 10 _____ old.

2. There are 30 _____ in June.

3. Nancy's baby brother started to walk at the age of 11 _____.

4. We have 48 _____ in 2 days.

5. Nick's swimming lesson is 25 _____ long.

6. It took Leslie 10 _____ to comb her hair.

7. Mother's Day is celebrated once a _____.

8. Many children get about 3 _____ of summer vacation.

9. It takes about 1 _____ to blink your eyes.

10. Most children go to school 5 _____ a week.

Write these words in alphabetical order. Be sure to look at the third or fourth letters.

1. events, evening, every, eventually

_____ _____ _____ _____

2. tremendous, treatment, tree, treasure

_____ _____ _____ _____

3. coast, coconut, coal, collect, color

_____ _____ _____ _____ _____

4. entrance, entry, end, enthusiasm, enough

_____ _____ _____ _____ _____

5. grandfather, graph, grain, grateful, grab, graduated

_____ _____ _____ _____ _____ _____

What Does It Really Mean? An <u>idiom</u> is an expression whose meaning can't be understood by just knowing the individual words. Write what you think these idiomatic expressions mean.

1. She was really <u>pulling my leg</u>. _____

2. Do you think we'll <u>be in hot water</u>? _____

3. When you are having fun, <u>time flies</u>. _____

4. You've <u>hit it on the head</u>, Andrew. _____

5. Ryan will <u>lend a hand</u> tomorrow. _____

6. In the winter, my bedroom is <u>like an icebox</u>. _____

7. Mrs. Tune always has beautiful flowers; she <u>must have a green thumb</u>.

_____

A Litter Graph. Go on a "litter" walk. In a plastic bag, gather up litter as you go. Only pick up <u>safe</u> litter. Do not pick up needles, litter you are unsure of, or anything marked hazardous waste. When you are finished, bring it home. Categorize what you have found and display it in a bar graph.

Type of Litter	1	2	3	4	5	6	7	8	9	10	more than 10

Place Value Division Patterns. We know that 8 ÷ 2 = 4, so 80 ÷ 2 = 40, and 800 ÷ 2 = 400. Do the following division patterns.

1. 9 ÷ 3 = _____   90 ÷ 3 = _____   900 ÷ 3 = _____

2. 8 ÷ 2 = _____   80 ÷ 2 = _____   800 ÷ 2 = _____

3. 12 ÷ 4 = _____   120 ÷ 4 = _____   1200 ÷ 4 = _____

4. 6 ÷ 3 = _____   60 ÷ 3 = _____   600 ÷ 3 = _____

5. 30 ÷ 6 = _____   300 ÷ 6 = _____   3000 ÷ 6 = _____

6. 72 ÷ 8 = _____   720 ÷ 8 = _____   7200 ÷ 8 = _____

7. 32 ÷ 8 = _____   320 ÷ 8 = _____   3200 ÷ 8 = _____

8. 49 ÷ 7 = _____   490 ÷ 7 = _____   4900 ÷ 7 = _____

9. 56 ÷ 8 = _____   560 ÷ 8 = _____   5600 ÷ 8 = _____

10. 25 ÷ 5 = _____   250 ÷ 5 = _____   2500 ÷ 5 = _____

Look up the word <u>meet</u> in a dictionary. At the end of each sentence, write what part of speech (noun or verb) <u>meet</u> is. Then write the number for the meaning of the word <u>meet</u>.

EXAMPLE:

   I will <u>meet</u> you at three.   *Verb – 2*

1. Tomorrow we are going to have a track <u>meet</u>.   _____

2. I hope he doesn't <u>meet</u> with disaster.   _____

3. We need to <u>meet</u> the plane at seven P.M.   _____

4. He will have to <u>meet</u> the payments every month.   _____

5. It was nice to <u>meet</u> and talk with you yesterday.   _____

6. Are you going to <u>meet</u> your friends later?   _____

Someone or Something with Power. What is power? Choose something or someone with power. How do they have power? How did they get it? Could they lose it? Do they use it? How? Why? Do you have power? Yes you do! What are some of the powers that you have? What are some that you don't have that you would like to have?

FACTOID
Carrots used to be found in almost every color except orange.

SUPER STAR

Find the quotients and the remainders. Use a separate piece of paper to show your work.

EXAMPLE:

```
        12 R 2
    3) 38
      -3
        8
       -6
        2
```

1. 3) 95

2. 4) 47

3. 4) 85

4. 5) 58

5. 2) 65

6. 9) 100

7. 7) 79

8. 5) 57

9. 3) 37

10. 4) 87

Draw a line between the syllables. First, try to <u>remember</u> what you have learned about where to divide words. Then use a dictionary if you need more help.

EXAMPLE:

1. col/umn

2. harness

3. liveliness

4. inflate

5. gable

6. glorious

7. slashing

8. alphabet

9. understood

10. pigeon

11. soviet

12. jewelry

13. afraid

14. bicycle

15. generation

16. frozen

17. difficult

18. vegetable

19. tennis

20. kerosene

21. evidence

The next time you watch TV or read a magazine, look at the commercials or ads. In the boxes below, write down what you think is true about the commercials or ads and what you think is false.

What is the commercial or ad about?	TRUE	FALSE
	1.	1.
	2.	2.
	3.	3.
	4.	4.
	5.	5.

Conserving Energy. Recycling saves energy and natural resources. Besides recycling, how can we conserve energy? Write down ways to conserve energy with the following:

water _____

_____

lights _____

_____

heat _____

_____

electricity _____

_____

transportation _____

_____

buying things _____

_____

bathroom _____

_____

Write the fraction that describes the shaded section.

EXAMPLE:

1.
$\frac{1}{2}$

2. ___

3. ___

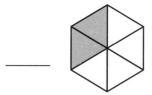

4. ___

5. ___

6. ___

7. ___

8. ___

9. ___

10. ___

11. ___

12. ___

Identify each angle and label it in the space below.

Right Angle—angle that measures 90 degrees (the angle forms a square corner)

Acute Angle—angle that measures less than a right angle, or less than 90 degrees

Obtuse Angle—angle that measures more than 90 degrees, or greater than a right angle

1. ___

2. ___

3. ___

4. ___

5. ___

6. ___

Practice writing and spelling these <u>homophones</u>. Write in cursive. After you know how to spell them, have someone give you a test to see if you can spell them without looking. Write each word twice.

way	_____	_____	tide	_____	_____
weigh	_____	_____	tied	_____	_____
base	_____	_____	waist	_____	_____
bass	_____	_____	waste	_____	_____
threw	_____	_____	sore	_____	_____
through	_____	_____	soar	_____	_____
scene	_____	_____	pare	_____	_____
seen	_____	_____	pair	_____	_____
sight	_____	_____	pear	_____	_____
site	_____	_____			

Water in the Air. There is water in the air. How does it get there? **Clouds and rain are made from water vapor in the air.**

Try this to help explain how water gets into the air. Take 3 or more drinking glasses that are all about the same size. Fill the glasses almost full of water. Place them in different areas, such as warm places, cool places, dark places, windy places, outside places, inside places, and other places of your choice. Watch them for 4 or 5 days or longer. Check the water levels. What happened to the water in the glasses? Where did it go? Explain in your own words where you think the water vapor in the atmosphere comes from and where it goes.

_____

_____

_____

_____

_____

_____

_____

Use the fraction table to help find out which fraction is greater and which fraction is less. Use >, <, or =.

1. $\frac{1}{2}$ ◯ $\frac{1}{4}$ 2. $\frac{2}{3}$ ◯ $\frac{1}{3}$

3. $\frac{1}{4}$ ◯ $\frac{1}{6}$ 4. $\frac{2}{6}$ ◯ $\frac{1}{3}$

5. $\frac{4}{8}$ ◯ $\frac{2}{10}$ 6. $\frac{1}{12}$ ◯ $\frac{1}{10}$

7. $\frac{3}{4}$ ◯ $\frac{2}{8}$ 8. $\frac{2}{5}$ ◯ $\frac{1}{3}$

9. $\frac{3}{8}$ ◯ $\frac{10}{12}$ 10. $\frac{2}{8}$ ◯ $\frac{1}{4}$

11. $\frac{1}{5}$ ◯ $\frac{2}{10}$ 12. $\frac{1}{3}$ ◯ $\frac{2}{4}$

13. $\frac{1}{6}$ ◯ $\frac{1}{3}$ 14. $\frac{3}{12}$ ◯ $\frac{1}{3}$

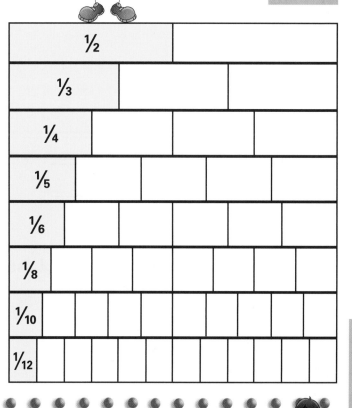

Write a short report. <u>Remember</u>: A report is only facts about a topic. Look in an encyclopedia for help. Follow these steps: Choose a topic and plan your report; then write, revise, proofread, and make a final copy.

These letters are in alphabetical order. See if you can make a word from them. The first letter is underlined.

EXAMPLE:

1. abbelopr _probable_

2. aaegimnz _____

3. aejlosu _____

4. eiorssu _____

5. eeenprrst _____

6. ghhottu _____

7. beeemmrr _____

8. irstw _____

9. beknnoru _____

10. aeginrv _____

11. cdffiilut _____

12. dinrstuy _____

13. accdginor _____

14. ceenrt _____

15. eegmnnortv _____

16. ehilstw _____

Put the letters in these words in alphabetical order.

17. creature _____

18. factory _____

19. fountain _____

20. hospital _____

21. basement _____

22. committee _____

● ●

Blow Up a Balloon. Here is an experiment that you can do in your home with an adult's permission. Get a balloon and blow it up several times until the balloon becomes easy to enlarge. Put one tablespoon of baking soda in the balloon; then put 3 tablespoons of white vinegar into a soda pop bottle. Now put the balloon opening around the mouth of the soda pop bottle. Move the balloon so the baking soda falls down and mixes with the vinegar. Draw a picture of what happens and write a couple of sentences to go with your picture.

Draw what happens!

_____
_____
_____
_____
_____
_____
_____
_____

Multiplying 3-digit numbers by 1-digit numbers.

EXAMPLE:
$$\begin{array}{r} {\scriptstyle 21} \\ 186 \\ \times\ 3 \\ \hline 558 \end{array}$$

6 x 3 = 18   3 x 80 = 240   3 x 100 = 300

18 + 240 + 300 = 558

1. 162
   x 5

2. 398
   x 2

3. 904
   x 8

4. 329
   x 5

5. 240
   x 7

6. 432
   x 6

7. 412
   x 8

8. 542
   x 9

9. 506
   x 5

10. 554
    x 6

11. 473
    x 9

12. 257
    x 8

Put commas in the following sentences to separate words in a series.

1. Nan Tom Julie and James are going to a movie.

2. Anne took her spelling reading and math books to school.

3. The snack bar is only open on Monday Tuesday Friday and Saturday.

4. Our new school flag is blue green yellow black and orange.

5. Women men children and pets enjoy sledding.

6. Have you ever seen baby kittens piglets or goslings?

Now write four sentences of your own. Name at least three people, sports, or foods in a series. Be sure to put in the commas.

7. _____

8. _____

9. _____

10. _____

FACTOID
The inside of a banana peel can be used to polish leather.

Parents and Family. What do you think your parents and family have in mind for your life? What do they want you to accomplish? What would they like to see you do? How do you feel about it? Think and write about it.

_____

_____

_____

_____

_____

_____

_____

_____

_____

_____

_____

_____

_____

_____

_____

_____

_____

_____

_____

How Many Times in a Minute? Use a stopwatch or a watch with a minute hand to time yourself as you do the following activities. Use that information to calculate how many times you could do those things in 5 minutes, 8 minutes, 10 minutes, and 15 minutes.

1. How far can you hop in a minute? _____

2. How far can you walk in a minute? _____

3. How many jumping jacks can you do in a minute? _____

4. How many times can you toss a ball and catch it in a minute? _____

5. How many times can you bounce a ball in a minute? _____

6. How many times do you breathe in a minute? _____

7. How many times can you write your name in a minute? _____

Activity	Minutes				
	1	5	8	10	15
hop					
walk					
jumping jacks					
toss and catch ball					
bounce ball					
breathe					
write name					

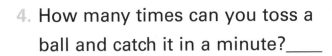

Put commas after <u>yes</u> or <u>no</u> when they begin a sentence and before and/or after names when that person is being spoken to. Put the commas in these sentences.

1. Yes I will go with you John.

2. Aaron do you play tennis?

3. Kirk do you want to go?

4. No Eli I never learned how.

5. No I need to finish this.

6. Come on T.J. let's go to the game.

7. John I am glad Sam will come.

8. Yes I was x-rayed at the doctor's.

9. Nicky what happened?

10. Mom thanks for the help.

11. Don I fell on the sidewalk.

12. Tell me Joe did you do this?

Do you know when the holidays come? Fill in the blanks with the date or name of the correct holiday. Use a calendar if you need help.

1. Many children look forward to _____ or _____ in December.
2. On January 1 we celebrate _____ _____ _____.
3. In May we have _____ _____.
4. Be sure to wear green in March. It's _____ _____ _____.
5. In October 1492 he sailed the ocean blue. _____ _____.
6. On February 14 be sure to send your sweetheart a _____.
7. On July 4 we celebrate _____ _____.
8. October 31 can be really scary. _____.
9. Sometimes it comes in March; sometimes it comes in April: _____.
10. Do you work on _____ _____ in September?
11. _____ and _____ also have birthdays in February.
12. In June we also have _____ _____.
13. Martin Luther King Jr.'s birthday is in _____.
14. Because the Pilgrims came, we have _____.
15. _____ _____ is in June.
16. On November 11 we honor our _____.

● ●

At the top of each page in a dictionary you will find two <u>guide</u> <u>words</u>. The guide word on the *left* tells you the first word found on the page. The guide word on the *right* tells you the last word on the page. Circle the word that will be found on the page with the following guide words.

1. bowling-brain

bread   braid   brawl

2. monster-mope

morbid   monsoon   moon

3. golem-gossamer

gondola   goal   gourd

4. flank-flaw

flash   flame   flight

5. liquid-litter

lists   live   lion

6. work-worst

word   world   worth

7. spoon-spread

spoil   sprite   spray

8. central-chafe

cell   chalet   certain

Draw a new figure by following the directions given.

1. Flip horizontally.

3. Flip vertically.

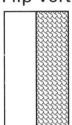

5. Flip vertically, turn 90°.

2. Turn 180° ($\frac{1}{2}$ turn).

4. Turn 90° ($\frac{1}{4}$ turn).

6. Turn 270° ($\frac{3}{4}$ turn).

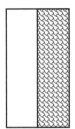

Using Punctuation Marks. Put periods and question, exclamation, and quotation marks in the following sentences. Use proper capitalization.

1. Nate, do you have the map of our town asked Kit

2. What an exciting day I had cried Mary

3. I said the puppy fell into the well

4. Did you learn that birds' bones are hollow asked Mrs. Tippy

5. She answered No, I did not learn that

6. Wayne exclaimed I won first prize for the pie eating contest

7. I'm tired of all work and no play said Sadie

8. I agree with you replied Sarah

9. Mr. Harris said this assignment is due tomorrow

10. It will be part of your final grade he added

Circle the two words in each group that are spelled correctly.

A	**B**	**C**	**D**	**E**
gabel	suger	allready	where	jackit
genuine	surpize	among	weather	junior
gracefull	terrible	aunte	wite	jujment
graine	straight	awhile	weare	justece
great	sonday	addvise	rotee	journey

F	**G**	**H**	**I**	**J**
rimind	feathers	donkiys	handsum	explore
remain	feever	doubble	herrd	elctrecity
fouff	finsih	drawer	holiday	enjine
refer	folow	dosen	healthy	enormous
raisd	fiction	detective	haevy	ecstat

Complete the picture and add any other details you would like.

Equal Fractions. Use the fraction table on page 59 to find equal fractions.

1. $\dfrac{1}{3} = \dfrac{}{6}$

2. $\dfrac{4}{5} = \dfrac{}{10}$

3. $\dfrac{10}{10} = \dfrac{}{6}$

4. $\dfrac{}{5} = \dfrac{4}{10}$

5. $\dfrac{4}{16} = \dfrac{}{8}$

6. $\dfrac{12}{12} = \dfrac{}{10}$

7. $\dfrac{3}{6} = \dfrac{}{12}$

8. $\dfrac{9}{12} = \dfrac{}{4}$

9. $\dfrac{}{12} = \dfrac{4}{6}$

10. $\dfrac{0}{4} = \dfrac{}{2}$

11. $\dfrac{6}{8} = \dfrac{}{4}$

12. $\dfrac{1}{2} = \dfrac{}{10}$

13. $\dfrac{}{4} = \dfrac{4}{8}$

14. $\dfrac{3}{9} = \dfrac{}{3}$

15. $\dfrac{}{15} = \dfrac{2}{3}$

16. $\dfrac{2}{3} = \dfrac{}{12}$

What Does It Mean? Choose a word from the Word Bank and write it next to the correct meaning.

Word Bank

- schedule
- assistant
- campaign
- approximately
- hollow
- exchange
- university
- venture
- artificial
- publicity
- reputation
- genuine

1. not natural, not real _____

2. a timed plan for a project_____

3. a giving or taking of one thing for another_____

4. esteem in which a person is commonly held_____

5. a person who serves or helps_____

6. really being what it is said to be; true or real_____

7. a series of organized, planned actions_____

8. to make information commonly known_____

9. near in position_____

10. an educational institution of the highest level_____

11. having a cavity within it, not solid_____

12. something on which a risk is taken_____

A <u>simile</u> is a figure of speech that compares one thing to another using the words <u>as</u> or <u>like</u>. For example: The bed sheets were as white as a snowy owl.

Complete the following similes.

1. The broken glass was lying on the ground like _____

   _____

2. Her eyes were like _____

   _____

3. The night was as dark as _____

4. His legs were as _____

5. The baby's cry was like _____

   _____

First-Aid Kit. Every home should have a first-aid kit. This enables the family to have many types of bandages and medicines in one place, should they be needed.

   Make a list of things you think should be in a first-aid kit. When you are finished, check with your parents to see if you have all the basic things listed for a first-aid kit. If your family has one, ask your parents to go through it with you.

_____

_____

_____

_____

_____

_____

_____

_____

_____

Adding Fractions.

$\frac{1}{3} + \frac{2}{3} = \frac{3}{3}$ ← add the numerator
← use the same denominator

1. $\frac{1}{3} + \frac{1}{3} =$ 2. $\frac{1}{2} + \frac{1}{2} =$ 3. $\frac{6}{12} + \frac{5}{12} =$ 4. $\frac{11}{12} + \frac{11}{12} =$

5. $\frac{5}{8} + \frac{2}{8} =$ 6. $\frac{3}{10} + \frac{4}{10} =$ 7. $\frac{1}{6} + \frac{2}{6} =$ 8. $\frac{7}{10} + \frac{6}{10} =$

9. $\frac{1}{4} + \frac{2}{4} =$ 10. $\frac{1}{8} + \frac{6}{8} =$ 11. $\frac{4}{9} + \frac{4}{9} =$ 12. $\frac{2}{8} + \frac{4}{8} =$

13. $\frac{3}{6} + \frac{1}{6} =$ 14. $\frac{4}{12} + \frac{5}{12} =$ 15. $\frac{3}{8} + \frac{3}{8} =$ 16. $\frac{8}{12} + \frac{5}{12} =$

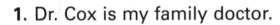

Circle the <u>abbreviations</u> in these sentences.
<u>Remember:</u> **Abbreviations are short forms of words and usually begin with capital letters and end with periods.**

1. Dr. Cox is my family doctor.

2. Do you live on Rocksberry Rd.?

3. My teacher's name is Ms. Hansen.

4. On Mon. we are taking a trip to Fort Worth, Tx.

5. Will Mr. Harris sell his company to your parents?

Now write the abbreviations for these words.

6. avenue _____   **7.** Tuesday _____

8. postscript _____   **9.** Mister _____

10. teaspoon _____   **11.** tablespoon _____

12. January _____   **13.** circle _____

14. Thursday _____   **15.** company _____

Choose 4 <u>compound</u> <u>words</u> and illustrate them.

EXAMPLE: <u>super</u>market is <u>super</u> and <u>market</u>.

Here are some to choose from, or you can choose some of your own: billfold, screwdriver, backyard, butterfly, rainbow, drawbridge, postman, undertake, windpipe, starfish, basketball.

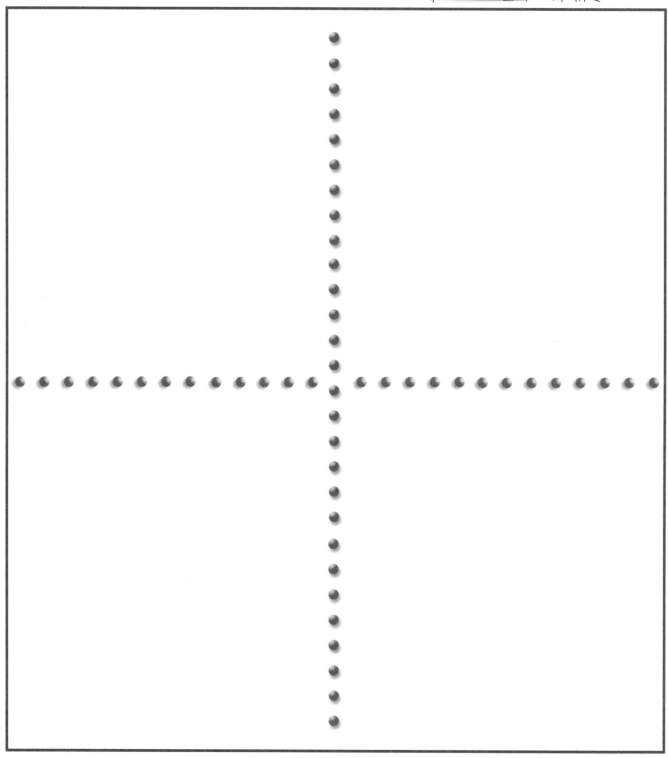

Understanding Polygons.

Closed figures that have straight lines are *polygons*.
Which of these are polygons? _____

1. 　2. 　3. 　4. 　5.

Why? _____

Where each side or point meets is called a *vertex*. Count and write the number of sides and the number of vertices each polygon has.

　　triangle　　　　　pentagon　　　　quadrilateral　　　　octagon

sides _____　sides _____　sides _____　sides _____

vertices _____　vertices _____　vertices _____　vertices _____

How are these shapes below alike? _____

How are they different? _____

• •

Write the book titles correctly. <u>Remember:</u> Underline the whole title and use capital letters at the beginning of all the important words and the last word in the title.

1. millions of cats _____

2. higher than the arrow _____

3. john paul jones _____

4. no flying in the house _____

5. ludo and the star horse _____

6. an elephant is not a cat _____

7. one wide river to cross _____

8. the polar express _____

9. where the sidewalk ends _____

Neighborhood Survey. Conduct a survey with your neighborhood, friends, or relatives. Find out how many have pets. If possible, observe them with their pets. Do they keep their pets inside or outside? Are the pets left to find their own food or part of their food, or is their food provided for them? How much space do they have to move around in? Think of other questions you might ask. Record your information in a report, chart, graph, table, or picture.

Use what you know about polygons to make a pattern. Start with one polygon and flip, turn, or slide it to make a pattern.

EXAMPLE:

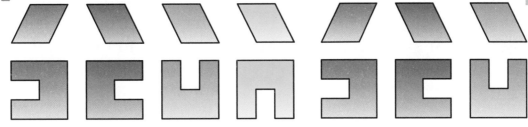

or

Now try your hand at making some polygon patterns.

Review of Homonyms or Homophones. Write 5 sentences using some of these pairs of homonyms or homophones. Be sure to use both words and underline them.

EXAMPLE: <u>Would</u> you chop some <u>wood</u>?

1. no, know	**2.** four, for	**3.** way, weigh
4. ate, eight	**5.** sun, son	**6.** sent, cent
7. see, sea	**8.** tail, tale	**9.** rode, road
10. knight, night	**11.** sale, sail	**12.** pair, pear
13. new, knew	**14.** so, sew	**15.** their, there

_____

_____

_____

_____

_____

_____

_____

_____

_____

_____

Read this paragraph. Put in the punctuation marks that are missing. Don't forget capitals.

do you ever wonder about the planet pluto it takes pluto 248 earth years to orbit the sun most of the time pluto is farther away from the sun than any other planet but for some time pluto had been closer to the sun than neptune because it was traveling inside neptune's orbit it remained in neptunes orbit until february 9 1999 pluto is now traveling out of neptunes orbit

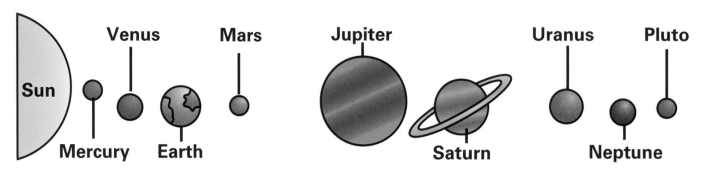

See if you can find more information about Pluto. Did you know that some astronomers believe that it was once a moon of Neptune? Look in an encyclopedia to find out more.

Chart the weather and temperature for the month. You will need to check with the weatherman for the high and low temperatures for the day. Write down or draw the weather for the day. Include the high and low temperature.

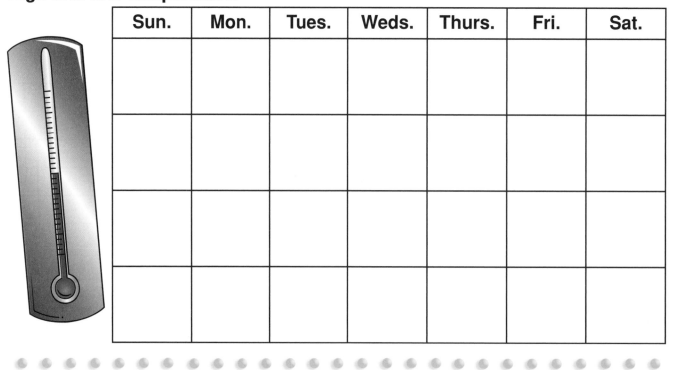

Sun.	Mon.	Tues.	Weds.	Thurs.	Fri.	Sat.

Rename these fractions.

EXAMPLE:

1. $\frac{5}{4} = 1\frac{1}{4}$ 2. $\frac{10}{3} =$ 3. $\frac{9}{8} =$ 4. $\frac{8}{3} =$

5. $\frac{5}{2} =$ 6. $\frac{7}{4} =$ 7. $\frac{10}{3} =$ 8. $\frac{11}{10} =$

9. $\frac{10}{7} =$ 10. $\frac{19}{8} =$ 11. $\frac{25}{10} =$ 12. $\frac{9}{5} =$

13. $\frac{31}{10} =$ 14. $\frac{23}{10} =$ 15. $\frac{17}{8} =$ 16. $\frac{13}{3} =$

Name the parts of a letter.

1 _____

2 _____

3 _____

4 _____

5 _____

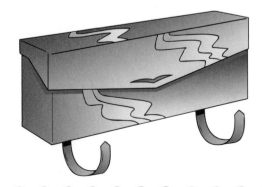

1
1624 Oak Avenue
Amarillo, TX 79103
June 20, 1995

2 Dear Pat,

3
  Today my friends and I went swimming in June's pool. We had a lot of fun.
  I sure miss you. I wish your family hadn't moved. Have you made any new friends yet?
  Please write to me as soon as you can.

4 Your friend,

5 Judy

Complete each sentence by circling the word that is spelled correctly; then write it in the blank space. Use a dictionary if necessary.

1. The big cat couldn't _____ from the trap.
   a. escape   b. iscape   c. eskape   d. acape   e. iccape

2. Mother paid $100.00 for _____.
   a. groseries   b. groceeries   c. groceries   d. grcerees   e. grooseries

3. Anna is a very _____ person.
   a. kreative   b. creative   c. createive   d. crative   e. creetive

4. Have you ever seen a more _____ man?
   a. handsum   b. hansome   c. handsume   d. handcome   e. handsome

5. We love to _____ ride in the winter.
   a. sleigh   b. sleia   c. cleigh   d. slagh   e. sleeigh

6. I found the perfect _____ for my new dress.
   a. matterial   b. matirial   c. metariel   d. material   e. materiall

7. Scott's son got a _____ to Harvard University.
   a. schoolarship b. scholarship c. skullarship d. sholarship e. scholership

8. What would it take to _____ your appetite?
   a. satesfy   b. satisfi   c. satisffy   d. catisfy   e. satisfy

9. Richard, turn down the _____!
   a. volime   b. volumee   c. volume   d. volumme   e. valume

10. That was a _____ report, Amy.
    a. fantistic   b. fantastik   c. fanntastic   d. fantastic   e. fantestic

Electricity. Make a list of all the things around you that use electricity.

_____

_____

_____

_____

_____

_____

_____

_____

_____

_____

_____

Rock Candy Crazy!

Rock candy is yummy! (Maybe not so good for the teeth, but yummy!)

Stuff You Need: (adult supervision)

water   cotton string   drinking glass
food coloring (optional)   masking tape   pencil
saucepan (nonstick, 4-quart)   stove top   sugar

Here's What to Do:

1. When starting with this solution, be sure to leave at least two-thirds of the saucepan empty. This leaves enough room for the sugar to dissolve and displace the water.

2. Have an adult help you use the stove. Fill your pan a little less than one-third full with water. Set it on the stove top to boil. When the water is boiling, slowly add the sugar. Stir the solution so the crystals dissolve more quickly. Add twice as much sugar as you have water to get a pan of syrup.

3. Once the syrup is made, wet the cotton string in water. Then roll it in dry sugar. This "seeds" the string and gives the sugar in the solution something to hang on to. Tie the string to a pencil and hang it in your glass so it just touches the bottom of the glass.

4. The syrup can now be added to the glass. Fill it close to the top. If you want colored rock candy, add a bit of food coloring to the syrup. Gently swirl it around.

5. Set the glass in a place where it will not be bothered. Don't pull the string out of the solution to look at it. This disrupts the crystal formation. You will also want to place a paper towel over the glass because ants love this experiment, and they may troop through your house to find it! Also, bacteria and dust may get in an uncovered glass.

6. The crystals may take one or two weeks to form. How long it takes depends on how sugary the syrup is and the number of seeds on the string. When the crystals have formed, you can eat this sweet concoction of pure sugar.

What's This All About?

One of the basic concepts of science is conservation of energy. This means that all things use up the least amount of energy possible. A water molecule in the gas state moves all over the place. This takes a lot of energy. It would take a lot less energy if the water molecule were a liquid, so the water vapor condenses into a water droplet. If the temperature drops low enough, the liquid can turn into a solid, becoming a piece of ice or a snowflake. This is conservation of energy.

Sugar is usually found as a solid at room temperature. When it is in the liquid form it takes extra energy for it to remain so. Since conservation of energy is the key, the sugar tries to recrystallize. When you pour the solution into the glass, the sugar molecules cling to the string to recrystallize. As more and more sugar molecules hang on, the crystals start to form.

Lung Capacity!

Take a deep breath! Hold it . . . hold it . . . Whoosh! Let it all out. Now, how much air was in your lungs? Here's how to find out.

Stuff You Need:

marker (permanent)
metric measuring cup
soda bottle (2-liter)
tub (large, plastic)
tubing (rubber)
water

Here's What to Do:

1. Put 250 ml of water into the bottle and make a mark. Continue to fill the bottle with 250 ml at a time, making a mark for each new level of water until you reach the 2 liter mark and the bottle is full.

2. Add 2 inches of water to the tub. Stick one end of the tubing inside the soda bottle. The other end should hang over the side of the tub. Quickly flip the bottle upside down and set the opening in the tub of water so that no water pours out.

3. Take a deep breath and blow all the air in your lungs into the tube. Your breath will push water into the tub as long as you are blowing into the tubing.

4. When you run out of air, quickly flip the bottle right side up to see how much air you added. See how far down the new water line is from the old water line. This amount is a rough measurement of your lung capacity!

5. Have other people try the same experiment and record their lung capacities on a Record Sheet like the one at the bottom of this page.

Lung capacity varies with size as well as with physical fitness. So it's OK if others' results are different!

Record Sheet

Name _____

Amount of water displaced _____ ml

My lung capacity is _____ml.

Motivational Calendar

Month _____

My parents and I decided that if I complete
15 days of **Summer Bridge Activities**™ and
read _____ minutes a day, my incentive/reward will be:

_____

Child's Signature _____ Parent's Signature_____

Day 1	☆	📖	_____	Day 9	☆	📖	_____
Day 2	☆	📖	_____	Day 10	☆	📖	_____
Day 3	☆	📖	_____	Day 11	☆	📖	_____
Day 4	☆	📖	_____	Day 12	☆	📖	_____
Day 5	☆	📖	_____	Day 13	☆	📖	_____
Day 6	☆	📖	_____	Day 14	☆	📖	_____
Day 7	☆	📖	_____	Day 15	☆	📖	_____
Day 8	☆	📖	_____				

Child: Color the ☆ for daily activities completed.
Color the 📖 for daily reading completed.

Parent: Initial the _____ when all activities are complete.

Discover Something New!

Fun Activity Ideas to Go Along with Section Three!

 1. Draw a picture of your favorite friend, toy, or teacher in your favorite time of the year.

 2. Put together a collection of leaves from your neighborhood and label as many as you can.

 3. Write five questions that you would like to ask the President of the United States.

 4. Invent a new ice cream flavor. How is it made? What will you call it?

 5. Play football with a Frisbee.

 6. Find out how to recycle in your town; then make and deliver flyers to inform all your neighbors.

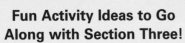

 7. Using a book on astronomy, look for stars and constellations. This is a fun nighttime activity.

 8. Write your answer to the following question: How would the world be different without Alexander Graham Bell?

 9. Surprise your parents and weed a flower bed or garden, rake the leaves, do the dishes, etc.

 10. Pretend you live in the year 2028. How will life be different? How will you look? What will you eat? How will you get around? Write it down and draw it.

 11. Play flashlight tag tonight!

 12. Design a comic strip and draw it.

 13. Paint a mural on butcher paper.

 14. Set up a miniature golf course in your own backyard.

 15. Play hockey using a broom.

Add and rename fractions where needed.

EXAMPLE:

1. $\frac{3}{4} + \frac{2}{4} = \frac{5}{4}$ or $1\frac{1}{4}$

2. $\frac{6}{10} + \frac{8}{10} =$

3. $\frac{3}{4} + \frac{5}{4} =$

4. $\frac{9}{11} + \frac{2}{11} =$

5. $\frac{10}{12} + \frac{14}{12} =$

6. $\frac{6}{11} + \frac{7}{11} =$

7. $\frac{7}{12} + \frac{8}{12} =$

8. $\frac{6}{8} + \frac{5}{8} =$

9. $\frac{5}{15} + \frac{10}{15} =$

10. $\frac{9}{16} + \frac{9}{16} =$

11. $\frac{4}{7} + \frac{5}{7} =$

12. $\frac{8}{9} + \frac{6}{9} =$

Look at the letter on page 75 to answer the following questions.

1. What does the heading tell you? _____

_____

2. How many paragraphs are in the letter? _____

3. What is the signature? _____

_____

4. What words in the letter have capitals?_____

_____

_____

_____

5. Where are the commas in the letter? _____

_____

_____

_____

_____

Electric Circuit Crossword Puzzle.

Across

1. Electric currents from a battery flow in one direction from n _ _ _ _ _ _ _ _ to p _ _ _ _ _ _ _.

2. Electrical c _ _ _ _ _ _ means the flow of charged particles.

3. M _ _ _ _ _ are good conductors of electrical currents because electricity can flow through them easily.

4. The plastic or rubber coverings on wires are called i _ _ _ _ _ _ _ _ _ _.

5. In a lightbulb, when the switch is turned on or connected, the electricity flows through what we call a c _ _ _ _ _ c _ _ _ _ _ _.

6. When electricity flows through the wires on a toaster they become hot, and h _ _ _ from the wires toasts our bread.

7. L _ _ _ _ _ and thickness are the two things that determine the wires' resistance that causes them to become hot.

8. A _ _ _ _ _ _ _ _ _ _ such as electric stoves and toasters contain wires that are conductors of electricity.

9. A b _ _ _ _ _ _ is a cell storing an electrical charge and capable of furnishing an electrical current.

10. Copper and aluminum are good c _ _ _ _ _ _ _ _ _ of electricity because it can go through them easily due to their low resistance to the electrical current.

Down

1. A r _ _ _ _ _ _ _ _ is a tool used to control the amount of electrical current that goes through a circuit.

2. When wires, bulbs, and batteries are connected they make a path for electricity to flow through called an e _ _ _ _ _ _ _ _ _ _ c _ _ _ _ _ _.

3. Lightbulbs have a special wire in them called a f _ _ _ _ _ _ _.

4. The property of the filament that makes it light up when electricity flows through it is called the r _ _ _ _ _ _ _ _ _ to electricity.

Subtracting Fractions.

$\frac{4}{5} - \frac{1}{5} = \frac{3}{5}$ ← subtract the numerators
← keep the same denominators

1. $\frac{2}{6} - \frac{1}{6} =$

2. $\frac{5}{10} - \frac{3}{10} =$

3. $\frac{3}{4} - \frac{2}{4} =$

4. $\frac{6}{8} - \frac{3}{8} =$

5. $\frac{8}{11} - \frac{3}{11} =$

6. $\frac{6}{7} - \frac{4}{7} =$

7. $6\frac{8}{10}$
$-3\frac{4}{10}$

8. $8\frac{4}{10}$
$-3\frac{3}{10}$

9. $7\frac{2}{5}$
$-3\frac{1}{5}$

10. $13\frac{3}{4}$
$-9\frac{1}{4}$

11. $14\frac{10}{12}$
$-7\frac{9}{12}$

12. $24\frac{7}{10}$
$-12\frac{3}{10}$

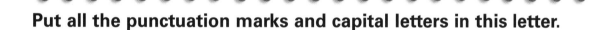

Put all the punctuation marks and capital letters in this letter.

Mr. Greg Jones
1461 Condor St.
Lake Tona, OH 12345

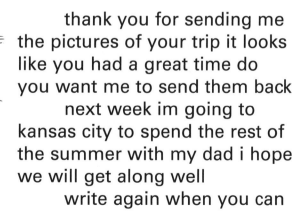

1461 condor st
lake tona oh 12345
july 21 1995

dear david

thank you for sending me
the pictures of your trip it looks
like you had a great time do
you want me to send them back
next week im going to
kansas city to spend the rest of
the summer with my dad i hope
we will get along well
write again when you can

your friend

greg

Use the words in the Word Bank to complete these sentences on "body facts."

FACTOID
The name "zipper" came from the sound a zipper makes when it is opened or closed.

Word Bank

- brain
- water
- calcium
- circulatory
- cells
- iron
- digestive
- eyes
- heart

1. Our bodies are made up of millions of tiny _____.

2. Our bodies are mostly _____, between 55 and 75 percent.

3. Our bodies have lots of metals and minerals in them, some of which are _____ and _____.

4. Our bodies have several systems that work together to help us. Our heart, blood vessels, and blood are part of our _____ system, which moves blood throughout our bodies.

5. Our salivary glands, esophagus, stomach, gallbladder, large intestines, and small intestines are part of our _____ system.

6. Our _____ is like a wonderful tool. It tells our _____ to beat and our _____ to blink.

A **synonym** is a word that means the same as another word. An **antonym** is a word that means the opposite of another word. Using a thesaurus, write a synonym and an antonym for each word below

1. rough _____

2. problem _____

3. winter _____

4. spring _____

5. mad _____

6. harvest _____

7. huge _____

8. inaccurate _____

9. calm _____

10. riot _____

Thesaurus

Addition and Subtraction with Thousands.

1. 5,162	2. 9,252	3. 7,825	4. 3,529
− 2,678	− 5,003	− 3,148	+ 7,506

5. 8,929	6. 9,341	7. 2,629	8. 4,528
+ 4,050	− 6,037	+ 7,536	+ 1,257

9. 7,932	10. 9,826	11. 4,723	12. 3,872
− 5,847	+ 1,329	+ 5,297	− 1,799

Write a letter to a friend, grandparent, or someone else you would like to write. Be sure to put in all five parts of the letter.
Remember: Letter writing uses the same steps as writing a story. Refer to page 59. Copy your letter to another sheet of paper.

Below are the stressed syllables of some spelling words. Fill in the missing syllables and then write the words in cursive. Each blank stands for a letter. The first one is done for you.

several	busy	accept	violin
~~parent~~	begin	dial	bacon
salad	wonderful	unlock	vegetable
library	limit	into	depend

1. par´ _ent_   _parent_

2. li´ _ _ _ _ _   _____

3. lim´ _ _   _____

4. in´ _ _   _____

5. _ _ pend´   _____

6. ba´ _ _ _   _____

7. di´ _ _   _____

8. _ _ gin´   _____

9. sev´ _ _ _ _   _____

10. sal´ _ _   _____

11. won´ _ _ _ _ _ _   _____

12. _ _ lock´   _____

13. veg´ _ _ _ _ _ _   _____

14. _ _ _ lin´   _____

15. _ _ cept´   _____

16. bus´ _   _____

Self-Portrait Poem.

1. Write your name.
2. Write two words that tell about you.
3. Write three words that tell what you like to do.
4. Write two more words that describe you.
5. Write your name again.

Try writing another "portrait poem" about a person or pet in your life.

_____   _____

_____   _____

_____   _____

_____   _____

_____   _____

_____   _____

_____   _____

It's about Time! <u>Remember:</u> There are 24 hours in a day. The times from midnight to noon are written a.m., and the times from noon to midnight are written p.m. Write down the times. Remember a.m. and p.m.

1.

2.

3.

_____ _____ _____

4. Write the time 50 minutes later than clock 1. _____

5. Write the time 25 minutes earlier than clock 2. _____

6. Write the time 95 minutes later than clock 3. _____

7. How much earlier is clock 1 than clock 2? _____

8. How much later is clock 3 than clock 2? _____

9. If you add 12 hours to clock 1, what time is it? _____

10. What was the time 6 hours earlier on clock 2? _____

This envelope is not addressed correctly. Rewrite it correctly. <u>Remember:</u> The <u>return address</u> is the address of the person writing the letter, and the <u>address</u> is the address of the person to whom the letter is going.

1461 condor st
mr greg jones
lake tona oh
12345

mr david fisher
little creek id
route 2 box 3 f

Who Did It?

Grayson and Matt were playing tennis in Matt's backyard with some friends. They had been playing all afternoon in the hot sun.

Matt decided that he was tired of playing tennis. He sat down on the back steps to watch the others. "Man, am I thirsty," he said. "I'm going in the house to get a drink." Several of the others decided that they were thirsty and went inside with Matt. "Wait for me!" hollered Grayson. "I'm coming, too!"

The boys agreed to watch television instead of playing more tennis. Then the other guys thought they had better go home because it was close to dinnertime. Matt said he was hungry and was going to look in the kitchen for something to eat. Grayson ran after him to remind him that his mom said they were not to eat anything before dinner. About that time Matt's mother came into the kitchen to fix dinner. "Who ate all the hot dogs?" she exclaimed. "They were right here on the counter." Grayson and Matt looked at each other. "Not us, Mom," Matt said.

"Somebody must have. Do you have any clues?"

They started looking around for clues. The mud off their shoes had left tracks on the floor but had come nowhere near where Matt's mother had put the hot dogs. After their survey of the kitchen, they sat down to discuss the "case of the missing hot dogs." Then they heard what sounded like a satisfied meow from the den. The three of them walked into the den to find Tiger, the cat, finishing off the last hot dog. He licked both his paws clean and meowed loudly. "No wonder we didn't find any cat tracks in the kitchen where the hot dogs were," laughed Matt's mother. "Tiger always keeps his paws very clean, unlike some boys I know."

After reading this story, write down at least five things you know about Matt and Grayson.

1. _____

_____

2. _____

_____

3. _____

_____

4. _____

_____

5. _____

_____

Fractions to Tenths and the Decimal Equivalents for the Fraction.
Remember: When working with fractions that have a denominator of 10, you can write them as fractions in tenths, or you can use the decimal equivalent. Do this activity by writing each both ways.

EXAMPLE:

1. 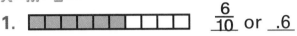 $\frac{6}{10}$ or .6

2. $\frac{3}{10}$ or ____.____

3. ____ or ____

4. $1\frac{7}{10}$ or ____.____

5. ____ or ____

6. $3\frac{5}{10}$ or ____.____

7. ____ or ____

8. 1.9 or ____

9. ____ or ____

10. .8 or ____

11. ____ or ____

12. 3.4 or ____

On page 85, you wrote a letter to someone. Today, address an envelope and send the letter to them. Be sure to put your address in the upper left-hand corner and the address of the person to whom you're sending the letter in the center. Don't forget to put a stamp in the upper right-hand corner. Use the space below to practice.

Write an <u>analogy</u> to finish these sentences. <u>Remember</u>: An analogy is a comparison between two pairs of words. Try to think of the relationship between the two words given and then think of another word that has the same kind of relationship to the third word.

EXAMPLE:

<u>Story</u> is to <u>read</u> as <u>song</u> is to _____**sing**_____.

1. <u>Brother</u> is to <u>boy</u> as <u>sister</u> is to _____.

2. <u>Princess</u> is to <u>queen</u> as <u>prince</u> is to _____.

3. <u>Milk</u> is to <u>drink</u> as <u>hamburger</u> is to _____.

4. <u>Arrow</u> is to <u>bow</u> as <u>bullet</u> is to _____.

5. <u>Car</u> is to <u>driver</u> as <u>plane</u> is to _____.

6. <u>Ceiling</u> is to <u>room</u> as <u>lid</u> is to _____.

7. <u>Paper</u> is to <u>tear</u> as <u>glass</u> is to _____.

8. <u>Large</u> is to <u>huge</u> as <u>small</u> is to _____.

9. <u>Wrist</u> is to <u>hand</u> as <u>ankle</u> is to _____.

10. <u>Father</u> is to <u>uncle</u> as <u>mother</u> is to _____.

11. <u>Cupboard</u> is to <u>dishes</u> as <u>library</u> is to _____.

12. <u>Hard</u> is to <u>difficult</u> as <u>easy</u> is to _____.

Exercising Parts of the Body. Make a list of 5 or 6 exercises. Some examples are running, hopping, sit-ups, jumping jacks, touching your toes, push-ups, jumping, skipping, playing sports, gymnastics, and swinging your arms. Try them. Which parts of the body are affected? Write down the results. Try this exercise. Take an ordinary spring-centered clothespin. Hold the ends between your thumb and one of your fingers. How many times can you open and close it in 30 seconds?

_____

_____

_____

_____

_____

_____

_____

Use what you know about <u>fractions to tenths</u> and their <u>decimal equivalents</u> to work with <u>hundreds</u>. **Remember:** When a whole object is divided into 100 equal parts, each part is <u>one hundredth</u> ($\frac{1}{100}$ or .01). Write the fraction as a decimal. The first one is done for you.

1. $\frac{49}{100}$ = .**49**

2. $\frac{25}{100}$ = .____

3. $\frac{20}{100}$ = .____

4. $\frac{86}{100}$ = .____

5. $\frac{37}{100}$ = .____

6. $\frac{9}{100}$ = .____

Now write the mixed number as a decimal.

7. $1\frac{93}{100}$ = ____.____

8. $7\frac{15}{100}$ = ____.____

9. $15\frac{47}{100}$ = ____.____

10. $46\frac{89}{100}$ = ____.____

11. $35\frac{6}{100}$ = ____.____

12. $625\frac{12}{100}$ = ____.____

13. $12\frac{5}{100}$ = ____.____

14. $81\frac{1}{100}$ = ____.____

15. $10\frac{11}{100}$ = ____.____

<u>**Adjectives**</u> are words that tell about or describe nouns and pronouns. Circle the adjective(s) in these sentences. Write the noun(s) or pronoun(s) described at the end of the sentences.

1. A (beautiful) light flashed across the (cloudy) sky. *light   sky*

2. On the tall mountain we found blue and yellow flowers._____

   _____

3. He was brave after the accident. _____

4. It is fun, but it is also dangerous to skydive. _____

5. Our brown dog had six cute puppies. _____

   _____

Now fill in the blanks with adjectives.

6. My _____ pencil is never in my desk.

7. The _____ students were having a _____ time.

8. The _____, _____ ride was making me sick.

9. My brother, Jack, sang a _____ song when we were camping.

10. _____, _____ snakes were wiggling around in the box.

Maintaining Good Health. Fill in the blanks with the following health terms: <u>nutrients</u>, <u>healthy</u>, <u>sleep</u>, <u>exercise</u>, <u>liquids</u>, <u>water</u>, <u>cleanliness</u>, <u>checkups</u>, <u>energy</u>, <u>food groups</u>. Some terms are used more than once.

1. _____ are basic nourishing ingredients in good foods that you eat.

2. _____ helps you to strengthen your muscles. It helps your heart and lungs grow, too.

3. _____ help you prevent tooth decay and maintain good health.

4. Meat, fruits, vegetables, milk, and breads and cereals make up the basic _____ _____ that keep you healthy.

5. Being healthy means feeling good and having the _____ to work and play.

6. Vitamins and minerals are kinds of _____ that you get from food.

7. Being _____ means feeling good and not being sick.

8. Sugar, starch, and fats are _____ that your body uses for fuel to give you _____.

9. You need to drink a lot of _____ because your body is approximately 60–70% _____.

10. Plenty of _____ helps give your body time to grow and repair itself. Children need 10 to 11 hours of it because they are still growing.

11. _____ is a way of fighting germs and staying healthy.

Are You Confused?

1. Are any of the lines curved? _____

2. Which vase is wider at the top and bottom? _____

3. Which line is longer, a or b?

_____

a.

b.

4. Is the hat taller than the brim is wide?

_____

**Decimals and Money. <u>Remember</u>: 100 pennies = 1 dollar.
One penny is 1/100 of a dollar, or $.01, so 49 pennies =
$.49. We can compute money by adding, subtracting,
multiplying, and dividing—just watch the decimals. Look at
the signs. Use a separate piece of paper to show your work.**

EXAMPLE:

```
   $57.34        $62.89         $12.45          $ 3.95
 + 62.89       - 34.91         x    3      5)$19.75
 _____      _____        _____        - 15
 $120.23       $27.98          $37.35          47
                                             - 45
                                               25
                                             - 25
                                                0
```

1. $409.75
  − 249.83
  _____
  $.

2. $14.74
  x   3
  _____
  $.

3. $492.00
  − 349.50
  _____
  $.

4. $.
  4)$12.92

5. $162.49
  + 186.32
  _____
  $.

6. $.
  7)$49.77

7. $601.89
  + 403.23
  _____
  $.

8. $9.57
  x   6
  _____
  $.

9. $668.45
  + 171.63
  _____
  $.

10. $915.04
  − 102.56
  _____
  $.

11. $741.13
  x   8
  _____
  $.

12. $.
  4)$29.48

Write <u>nouns</u> to go with these adjectives. The first one is done for you.

1. two red _apples_

2. fancy little _____

3. fluffy yellow _____

4. small pink _____

5. cold, wet _____

6. smooth green _____

7. dark, strange _____

8. fat, juicy _____

9. wild, dangerous _____

10. loud, shrill _____

11. furry black _____

12. fourteen blue _____

13. big, heavy _____

14. long, thick _____

Add a <u>prefix</u> and a <u>suffix</u> to the following words; then choose five of the words and write sentences with them.

suffix

prefix

1. _____ print _____
2. _____ spell _____
3. _____ light _____
4. _____ lock _____
5. _____ poison _____
6. _____ port _____
7. _____ courage _____
8. _____ cook _____
9. _____ agree _____
10. _____ appoint _____

Sentences:

1. _____
   _____
2. _____
   _____
3. _____
   _____
4. _____
   _____
5. _____
   _____

What's for Breakfast, Lunch, and Dinner? This is your day to plan the meals. You can have anything you want to eat for the day. It can be for the whole family or just yourself. Plan and write down your menu for breakfast, lunch, and dinner. You can even schedule a few snacks.

_____
_____
_____
_____
_____
_____
_____

Multiplying Multiples of 10 and 100.
To use shortcuts to find the product of multiples of 10 or 100, write the product for the basic fact and count the zeros in the factors.

10 x 8 = 80 (1 zero) **10 x 80 = 800** (2 zeros)   **10 x 800 = 8,000** (3 zeros)

Multiples of tens:

1. 10 x 5 = _____
2. 7 x 10 = _____
3. 39 x 10 = _____
4. 30 x 30 = _____
5. 54 x 10 = _____
6. 10 x 21 = _____
7. 710 x 10 = _____
8. 9 x 10 = _____
9. 70 x 30 = _____

Multiples of hundreds:

10. 900
    x 40

11. 600
    x 10

12. 230
    x 20

13. 700
    x 80

14. 500
    x 50

15. 600
    x 90

16. 440
    x30

17. 700
    x 60

Adjectives are used to compare. Add -er and -est to these adjectives.

EXAMPLE: red _____ *redder* _____ *reddest* _____

1. hot _____ _____ _____
2. nice _____ _____ _____
3. warm _____ _____ _____
4. hard _____ _____ _____
5. easy _____ _____ _____

Now write a story. Use as many of the adjectives above as you can. Underline the adjectives.

_____

_____

_____

_____

_____

_____

Choose 4 idioms and illustrate each one. Here are some to choose from, or you can use your own.

- Could you lend a hand?
- The boys were shooting the breeze.
- He's got rocks in his head.
- She gave him a dirty look.
- I got it straight from the horse's mouth.
- You won the game by the skin of your teeth.
- Time flies.
- Keep a stiff upper lip.
- She's a ball of fire.
- I'd really like to catch her eye.
- I was dog tired.

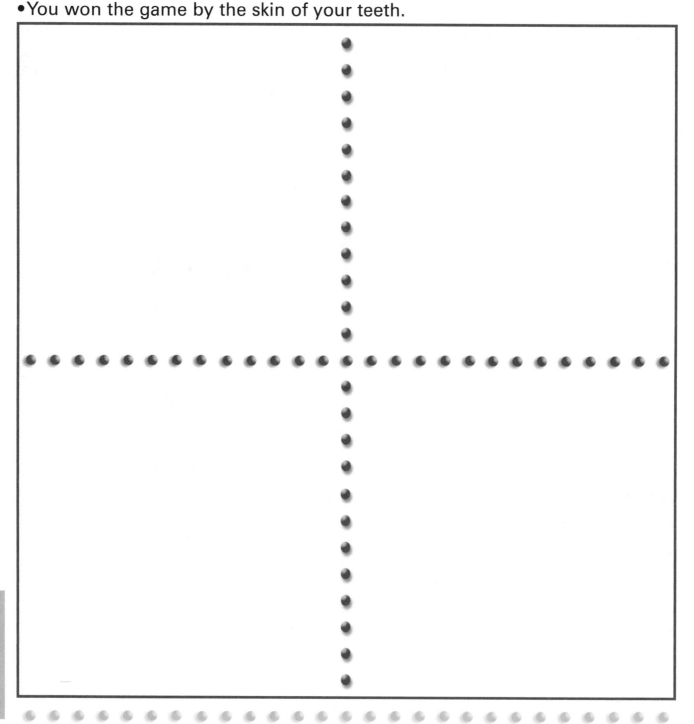

Place Value. A place-value chart can help you read as well as figure out large numbers.

Hundred Millions	Ten Millions	Millions	Hundred Thousands	Ten Thousands	Thousands	Hundreds	Tens	Ones
	8	6	5	3	7	1	4	3

Using the place-value chart to help you, read and write the following numbers. The first one is done for you.

1. Eighty-six million five hundred thirty-seven thousand one hundred forty-three **86,537,143** .

2. Seven hundred eighty-nine million four hundred ninety-six thousand three hundred twenty-one _____ .

3. One hundred sixty million seven hundred six thousand one hundred twenty-nine _____ .

4. Seventy-one million four hundred eleven thousand eight hundred ninety-nine _____ .

5. One hundred million three hundred seventy-five thousand _____ .

6. 1,369,000 _____

7. 375,403,101 _____

8. 894,336,045 _____

Overworked And. Rewrite the paragraph <u>and</u> leave out all the occurrences of <u>and</u> that you can. Write in cursive <u>and</u> be sure to put capitals <u>and</u> periods where they need to go.

My friend and I visited Cardiff, Wales, and we learned that Cardiff is the capital and largest port of Wales and the city lies on the River Taff near the Bristol Channel and Cardiff is near the largest coal mines in Great Britain and it is one of the great coal-shipping ports of the world.

_____

_____

_____

_____

How many times were you able to leave <u>and</u> out of the paragraph? _____

The following words are often misspelled. Write each word three times; then have someone give you a test. Use another piece of paper for your test.

EXAMPLE:

1. although _____ *although*   *although*   *although*

2. arithmetic _____

3. trouble _____

4. bought _____

5. chocolate _____

6. aunt _____

7. handkerchief _____

8. piece _____

9. vacation _____

10. practice _____

11. receive _____

12. getting _____

Categorizing the People in Your Family. Include some aunts, uncles, and cousins. Categorize them according to age, height, weight, hair color, hair length, eye color, etc. What do they have in common? What are some of their differences? Then draw a picture of them. Use a sheet of paper.

Family Member	Age	Height	Weight	Hair Color

Multiplying 2-Digit Numbers.

1. 39
    x 69

2. 72
    x 18

3. 85
    x 36

4. 23
    x 87

5. 46
    x 77

6. 57
    x 49

7. 41
    x 73

8. 48
    x 95

9. 88
    x 66

10. 68
    x 92

11. 507
    x 13

12. 456
    x 32

13. 640
    x 21

14. 576
    x 45

Write <u>S</u> by the word pairs that are synonyms, <u>A</u> by the word pairs that are antonyms, or <u>H</u> by the word pairs that are homonyms.

EXAMPLE:

tie • bind ___**S**___

high • low ___**A**___

here • hear ___**H**___

1. weep • cry ____

2. wonderful • terrible ____

3. look • glare ____

4. huge • large ____

5. away • toward ____

6. walk • stroll ____

7. never • always ____

8. bear • bare ____

9. ask • tell ____

10. cymbal • symbol ____

11. many • numerous ____

12. end • begin ____

13. hair • hare ____

14. move • transport ____

15. problem • solution ____

16. idea • thought ____

17. claws • clause ____

18. I'll • isle ____

19. add • subtract ____

20. try • attempt ____

21. that • this ____

22. doe • dough ____

23. enough • ample ____

24. board • bored ____

Read the clues to help you decide what words go in this crossword puzzle.

Down

1. birds with webbed feet
3. plays the piano
5. gave money
6. holds up the gate
8. boards for building
9. frilly
11. do it again to a story
12. hair by the eye
13. another name for a mule

Across

2. red from the sun
4. won't bend easily
5. eat outside
6. beginning of a word
7. decay of food
10. very large; great
14. nothing in it
15. cook in

• •

Think of one of your favorite fairy tales. Tell how the story begins, what happens in the middle, and how it ends. Write it in your own words and in the correct order. Don't write the whole story.

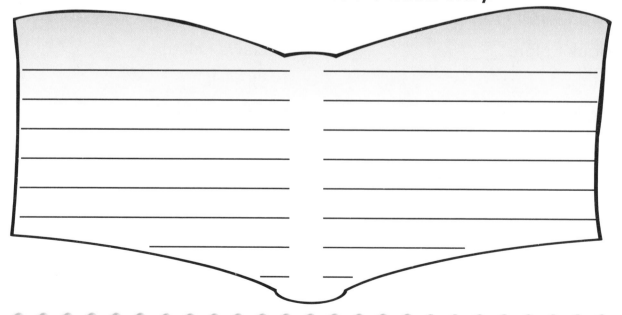

Quotients with Remainders. Use another sheet of paper if you need to.

EXAMPLE:

1. $20 \overline{) 48}$ **2 R8**
   $\quad\quad \underline{40}$
   $\quad\quad\quad 8$

2. $30 \overline{) 189}$

3. $70 \overline{) 456}$

4. $80 \overline{) 504}$

5. $30 \overline{) 281}$

6. $60 \overline{) 246}$

7. $90 \overline{) 458}$

8. $60 \overline{) 573}$

9. $40 \overline{) 172}$

10. $80 \overline{) 410}$

11. $60 \overline{) 692}$

12. $70 \overline{) 661}$

Equilateral Triangle—has three congruent sides
Isosceles Triangle—has only two congruent sides
Scalene Triangle—has no congruent sides

Classify the following triangles. Write <u>equilateral</u>, <u>isosceles</u>, or <u>scalene</u>.

1.
   _____

2.
   _____

3.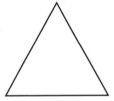
   _____

4.
   _____

5.
   _____

6.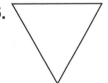
   _____

7.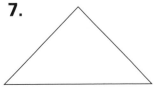
   _____

8.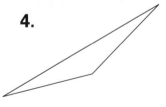
   _____

Adverbs Describe Verbs. Write an adverb to describe these verbs. Remember: Many adverbs end with -ly.

1. walk _quietly_
2. _____ run
3. smiled _____
4. _____ looked
5. painted _____
6. _____ cried
7. laughed _____
8. burned _____
9. arrived _____
10. went _____
11. folded _____
12. answered _____

Write five sentences using the verbs and adverbs you put together.

EXAMPLE: _I will walk quietly in the library._

13. _____
14. _____
15. _____
16. _____
17. _____

Make a "Happy" list and then a "Sad" list. Put the things that make you most happy at the top of your "Happy" list. Do the same thing with things that make you sad on your "Sad" list.

Happy List ☺   Sad List ☹

_____   _____
_____   _____
_____   _____
_____   _____
_____   _____
_____   _____

Multiplying Money. <u>Remember</u>: Multiply as you do using whole numbers and then place the decimal point or cents (2 numbers from the right).

EXAMPLE:

$.24	24 x 9 = 216
x 89	24 x 80 = 1920
216	1920 + 216 = 2136
+1920	
2136	Place the decimal and the dollar sign **$21.36**

1. $.65
   x 24

2. $.52
   x 36

3. $.94
   x 13

4. $.45
   x 25

5. $.81
   x 34

6. $.59
   x 54

7. $3.52
   x 34

8. $3.45
   x 56

- -

Perimeter—the distance around an object.

Measure the length of each side to find the perimeter in centimeters.

1.

_____ cm

2.

_____ cm

3.

_____ cm

4.

_____ cm

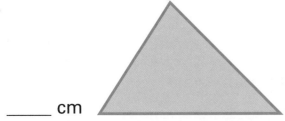

Read a book and fill out the following book report. Share it with a sibling or friend.

Title: _____

Author: _____

Illustrator: _____

Setting (where): _____

Main Characters (who): _____

Main Ideas (what): _____

_____

I liked the book because: _____

Tell which character in the book you would like to be and why: _____

Dictionary Sentences. Rewrite the following dictionary sentences using the correct spelling.

1. Thaŋk ū fôr thə yel´ō T shŭrt and blak shərts.

_____

2. Mis´tẽr Ralf livz ôn ə färm doun əlôŋ thə riv´ẽr.

_____

3. I stak´əd ôl thə kanz ôn top uv ēch uth´ẽr.

_____

4. Wē nēd ə gal´ən uv milk, sum egz, and but´ẽr, nou!

_____

Now rewrite these two sentences using the dictionary.

1. A thousand pennies equal ten dollars, I am told.

_____

2. Monkeys are funny, furry little animals in the zoo.

_____

Explain to an adult what the following geometrical terms mean. Show what each means by drawing an example of each.

1. Segments, lines, endpoints, and rays

2. Intersecting lines

3. Parallel lines

4. Perimeter

● ●

Adverbs tell <u>where</u>, <u>how</u>, or <u>when</u>. Tell what kind of adverb is underlined in the following sentences. Write <u>where</u>, <u>when</u>, or <u>how</u>.

1. Animals are <u>sometimes</u> called mammals. _____
2. There was a big accident on the freeway <u>yesterday</u>. _____
3. Joe <u>quickly</u> ran out to catch the bus. _____
4. We could hear the sound far <u>below</u> us. _____
5. Our campfire burned <u>brightly</u> all night. _____
6. We are going <u>there</u> next winter. _____
7. Be sure to write your letter <u>neatly</u>. _____
8. The birds will fly <u>away</u> if you scare them. _____

Now fill in the blanks with a <u>how</u>, <u>when</u>, or <u>where</u> adverb.

1. The car was going very (how) _____ .
2. Will you take April and June (where) _____ to the movie?
3. Mom will take them down (when) _____ .

Sometimes it's fun to share a story with someone else. Read a book; then call one of your friends or go visit them. Tell your friend about the book you read. Tell who the main characters are. Tell where the story takes place. Tell the plot or main event of the story. But don't tell them how the story ends. See if you can get them to read the book. On the rest of this page, write what happened. Did you get your friend to read the book?

_____

_____

_____

_____

_____

_____

It's important to know what the following words mean, especially when you're taking a test. Circle the letter that gives the best meaning for the underlined word in the sentence.

1. Can you <u>solve</u> this problem?
   a. copy   b. answer   c. recall
2. Make an <u>estimate</u> of how many people are in the U.S.
   a. approximate guess   b. count them   c. rank them
3. Let's take a <u>survey</u> of people who like red licorice.
   a. find out   b. examine   c. select
4. Will you <u>complete</u> your test in ten minutes?
   a. support   b. utilize   c. finish
5. Do <u>sections</u> one and two on this page.
   a. groups   b. parts   c. problems
6. Post office workers <u>classify</u> mail according to locations.
   a. change   b. write   c. arrange or group
7. We were pleased with our <u>survey</u> of the house.
   a. examination   b. explain   c. understanding
8. You will have to <u>prove</u> your answers.
   a. sample   b. question   c. to show as right and true
9. Do you understand the <u>directions</u>?
   a. why   b. describe it   c. how to do
10. Spencer <u>usually</u> knows the right answers.
    a. never   b. always   c. most of the time

More Geometry. Explain and draw an example of the following geometrical terms.

1. Congruent figures

2. Right angles

3. Triangles

4. Parallelograms

5. Polygons

1 pint (pt.) is equal to 2 cups.	1 gallon (gal.) is equal to 4 quarts.
1 quart (qt.) is equal to 2 pints.	1 pound (lb.) is equal to 16 ounces.

Circle the best answer or fill in the blank lines with the correct answer.

1. the capacity of a glass   2 cups   2 pt.   2 qt.   2 gal.
2. the capacity of a tub   60 cups   60 pt.   60 qt.   60 gal.
3. the capacity of a sink   2 cups   2 pt.   2 qt.   2 gal.
4. the capacity of a pitcher   2 cups   2 pt.   2 qt.   2 gal.

5. 5 pt. = _____ cups
6. 4 pt. = _____ qt.
7. 2 qt. = _____ pt.
8. 32 oz. = _____ lb.
9. 3 gal. = _____ qt.
10. 8 cups = _____ pt.
11. 5 lb. 8 oz. = _____ oz.
12. 4 pt. 1 cup = _____ cups
13. 4 qt. 1 pt. = _____ pt.
14. 16 qt. = _____ gal.
15. 5 pt. 1 cup = _____ cups
16. 12 pt. = _____ cups

Create small words from the letters in the following words. Write them.

EXAMPLE:
    borrow _____ *row*   *or*   *bow*   *rob*   *brow* _____

1. pajamas_____
2. carpenter_____
3. performance_____
4. bandage _____
5. knowledge _____
6. theory_____
7. satisfaction _____
8. customer _____
9. discovery_____
10. eventually _____
11. announcement _____
12. sentence _____

Sometimes things happen that cause something else to happen. This is called "cause and effect." A clue word helps to tell which is which. In the following sentences, underline the cause with a straight line (___). Underline the effect with a dotted line (_ _ _). Put a box ☐ around the clue word.

1. The tooth was broken, so it gave her a lot of pain.

2. The book was ripped and dirty because the dog got it.

3. Because it was so cold, Betty could ice skate for only a short while.

4. I went to bed early last night because I was so tired.

5. Because it was raining hard, we couldn't play outside.

6. The rabbit ran fast because the fox was after it.

7. It was very foggy out, so we could not see the mountains.

8. Because we got to the camp too late, there was no time for hiking.

9. It was very dark in the dugout, so we turned on the flashlight.

10. Kit played basketball too long after school; therefore, he missed the bus.

Graphs, Charts, and Tables. There are many different kinds of graphs, charts, and tables. Check your newspaper regularly to find different kinds and different information that you could chart or graph daily. This is a "broken-line" graph. Complete this graph using the information given in the table. Monday and Tuesday have been done for you.

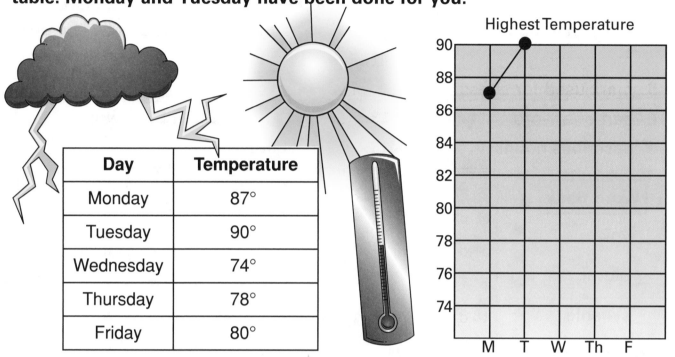

Day	Temperature
Monday	87°
Tuesday	90°
Wednesday	74°
Thursday	78°
Friday	80°

Highest Temperature

Write these sentences in the correct order. Underline the <u>negative word</u> in each sentence. The word that makes the sentence mean "no" or "not" is the negative word.

1. win won't contest I ever art an.

_____

2. involved does want be not He to.

_____

3. today I do have to no work more.

_____

4. nowhere play is us ball There for to.

_____

5. complains leg about never her She broken.

_____

6. ridden ever horse Jeremy a hasn't.

_____

Match the definitions below to a word in the Word Bank. Find and circle the words in the puzzle. The first one has been done for you.

1. ABC order
2. not a vowel
3. more than one
4. names things
5. mark used for stress
6. part of a word
7. describes nouns
8. used in place of a noun
9. just one
10. added to the beginning of a base word
11. describes verbs
12. not a consonant
13. added to the end of a base word
14. shows action

Word Bank

___vowel

___plural

___syllable

1 alphabetical

___consonant

___prefix

___adjectives

___nouns

___verb

___suffix

___pronoun

___adverbs

___accent

___singular

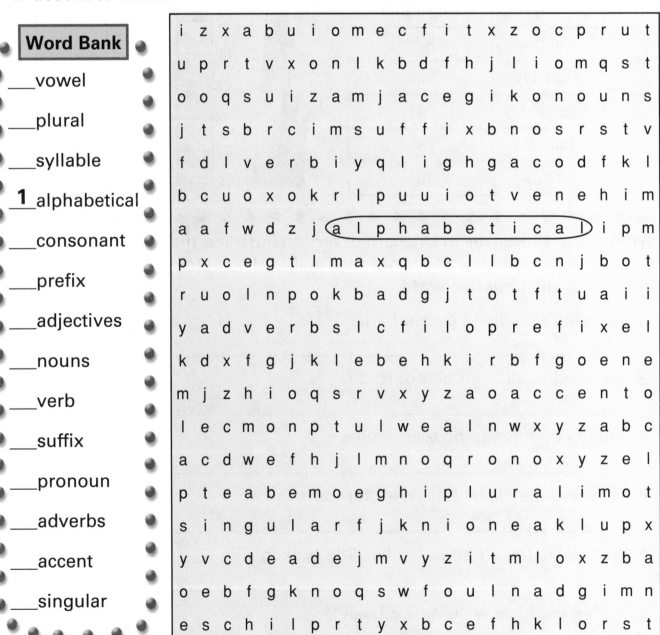

Rubber Bands and Steel Girders!

Do you know how your muscles work with your skeleton? The contraption you are getting ready to build demonstrates all the parts that help you move and bend.

Stuff You Need:

cardboard tubes (short) (2)
elastic cords (2)
marker (red)

chenille craft sticks (pipe cleaner)
hole punch
table tennis balls (2)

Here's What to Do:

1. With one hand, touch the hard places (bones) and the soft stuff (muscles) under the skin in your other arm from your elbow to your fingers. How many bones do you have in your lower arm? How many do you have in your leg from your knee to your toes?

2. Now, look carefully at a joint (where two bones come together) such as your elbow, knee, wrist, shoulder, or knuckle. Feel the backs of your knees and the top side of your elbows. You'll find stringy, cord-like things near these joints.

3. Punch four small holes in one end of each cardboard tube about three-fourths of an inch from the opening. The holes should be evenly spaced around the tube. Make sure the holes are big enough for the elastic cord and a chenille craft stick to slide through.

4. Slip one end of the elastic cord through holes on each side of one tube and continue through holes on each side of the second tube. Tie the cord loosely so you can hold the tubes apart about an inch without stretching the cord.

5. Place a table tennis ball between the tubes, as shown. The ball should fit snugly between the tubes, and the cord should be slightly stretched. You should be able to move the "bones" freely around the ball. Congratulations! You've just joined your bones with muscles, tendons, and cartilage. The tubes represent bones. The ball represents cartilage (a material that supports and cushions bones). The elastic cord represents both muscles and tendons (the stringy things that connect muscles to bones or cartilage).

6. Color the middle sections of the elastic cord with a red marker. The red parts of the cords are muscle, and the white parts are tendons. Muscles expand and contract (get larger and smaller), causing bones to move. To see how this happens, gather the "muscle" together on one side of the bones. This should cause the joint to bend toward the shorter muscle.

Notice that the muscle on the other side of the bones stretches in the opposite direction. Muscles in your body work in pairs. Those on one side of a joint get smaller while the ones on the other side get longer. To bend the bones the other way, the muscles that were stretching must contract, and the ones that were contracting must now stretch.

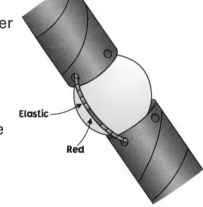

Elastic

Red

Swinging Water!

What would you say if someone told you to swing a bucket of ice-cold water over your head? Would you try it? You are going to have the opportunity to see just how brave you are!

Stuff You Need:

bucket with handle (a sand bucket works well if it has a strong handle)
water

Here's What to Do:

1. Go outside for this activity! If you goof indoors, you will have lots of cleanup to do. Not fun.

2. Fill the bucket about halfway with water.

3. Start swinging the bucket back and forth until you are making complete circles over your head (like a windmill) without spilling a drop.

What's This All About?

There are two forces keeping the water inside the bucket. The first one is **gravity**, and the second one is called **centrifugal force**.

Centrifugal force is created as an object swings rapidly in a circular motion. The object wants to travel in a straight line, but the handle keeps it going in a circle. This creates the force needed to keep the water in the bucket, even though it is completely upside down.

This is a good activity! And it shouldn't really be that messy if you are careful when you start and stop swinging.

What happened to the water in the bucket as you swung it upside down? _____

_____

What could you see? _____

_____

Imagine that you are swinging a clear bucket. Draw a picture of yourself swinging the bucket, and show what the water looks like inside the bucket when it is upside down.

Answer Pages

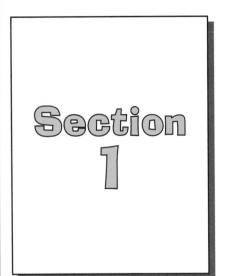

Section 1

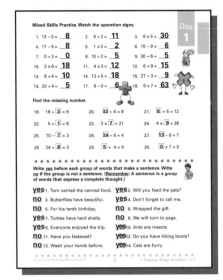

Page 3

Mixed Skills Practice. Watch the operation signs.

1. 13 − 5 = **8**   2. 9 + 2 = **11**   3. 6 × 5 = **30**
4. 17 − 9 = **8**   5. 1 × 2 = **2**   6. 8 − 9 = **6**
7. 0 × 0 = **0**   8. 30 + 6 = **5**   9. 30 ÷ 6 = **5**
10. 3 × 6 = **18**   11. 4 × 3 = **12**   12. 6 + 9 = **15**
13. 6 + 4 = **10**   14. 13 + 5 = **18** 15. 27 + 3 = **9**
16. 20 + 4 = **5**   17. 6 − 0 = **6**   18. 9 × 7 = **63**

Find the missing number.

19. 18 ÷ **3** = 6   20. **32** ÷ 4 = 8   21. **6** ÷ 6 = 12
22. 5 + **1** = 6   23. 3 × **7** = 21   24. 4 × **9** = 36
25. 10 − **7** = 3   26. **24** ÷ 6 = 4   27. **13** − 6 = 7
28. 24 ÷ **8** = 3   29. **5** ÷ 4 = 9   30. **0** × 7 = 0

Write yes before each group of words that make a sentence. Write no if the group is not a sentence. (Remember: A sentence is a group of words that express a complete thought.)

yes 1. Tom carried the canned food.   **yes** 2. Will you feed the pets?
no 3. Butterflies have beautiful.   **yes** 4. Don't forget to call me.
no 5. For his tenth birthday.   **no** 6. Wrapped the gift.
yes 7. Turtles have hard shells.   **no** 8. We will turn to page.
yes 9. Everyone enjoyed the trip.   **yes** 10. Ants are insects.
no 11. Have you fastened?   **yes** 12. Do you have hiking boots?
no 13. Wash your hands before.   **yes** 14. Cats are furry.

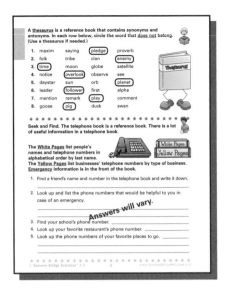

Page 4

A thesaurus is a reference book that contains synonyms and antonyms. In each row below, circle the word that does not belong. (Use a thesaurus if needed.)

1. maxim   saying   (pledge)   proverb
2. (folk)   tribe   clan   enemy
3. (time)   moon   globe   satellite
4. notice   (overlook) observe   see
5. daystar   sun   orb   (planet)
6. leader   (follower) first   alpha
7. mention   remark   (play)   comment
8. goose   (pig)   duck   swan

Seek and Find. The telephone book is a reference book. There is a lot of useful information in a telephone book.

The White Pages list people's names and telephone numbers in alphabetical order by last name.
The Yellow Pages list businesses' telephone numbers by type of business.
Emergency information is in the front of the book.

1. Find a friend's name and number in the telephone book and write it down.
2. Look up and list the phone numbers that would be helpful to you in case of an emergency.
Answers will vary.
3. Find your school's phone number.
4. Look up your favorite restaurant's phone number.
5. Look up the phone numbers of your favorite places to go.

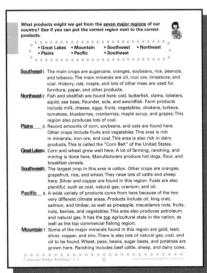

Page 5

Add or subtract these 3- or 4-digit numbers.

1. 681 + 145 = **826**   2. 428 − 119 = **309**   3. 4,918 + 3,928 = **8,846**   4. 2,830 − 519 = **2,311**
5. 248 + 48 = **296**   6. 569 − 247 = **322**   7. 2,709 + 1,282 = **3,991**   8. 6,219 − 4,356 = **1,863**
9. 304 − 172 = **132**   10. 143 + 219 = **362**   11. 3,744 − 1,378 = **2,366**   12. 7,645 − 564 = **7,081**

Add the correct word—their or there. Remember: their means "they own" or "have," and there means "in or at the place," or it can begin a sentence.

1. **There** must be something wrong with that cow.
2. The Hills were training **their** horse to jump.
3. We are going to **their** farm tomorrow.
4. Please put the boxes over **there**.
5. Will you please sit here, not **there**?
6. **Their** barn burned down yesterday.

Write four sentences about your school. Use their in two of them and there in the other two.

7.
8.
9.
10.
Sentences will vary.

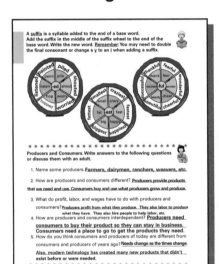

Page 6

A suffix is a syllable added to the end of a base word. Add the suffix in the middle of the suffix wheel to the end of the base word. Write the new word. Remember: You may need to double the final consonant or change a y to an i when adding a suffix.

Producers and Consumers. Write answers to the following questions or discuss them with an adult.

1. Name some producers. **Farmers, dairymen, ranchers, weavers, etc.**
2. How are producers and consumers different? **Producers provide products that we need and use. Consumers buy and use what producers grow and produce.**
3. What do profit, labor, and wages have to do with producers and consumers? **Producers profit from what they produce. They also labor to produce what they have. They also hire people to help labor, etc.**
4. How are producers and consumers interdependent? **Producers need consumers to buy their product so they can stay in business. Consumers need a place to go to get the products they need.**
5. How do you think consumers and producers of today are different from consumers and producers of years ago? **Needs change as the times change. Also, modern technology has created many new products that didn't exist before or were needed.**

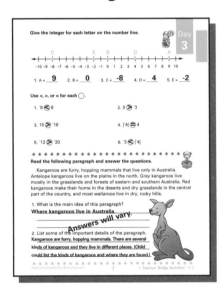

Page 7

Give the integer for each letter on the number line.

1. A = **9**   2. B = **0**   3. C = **-8**   4. D = **4**   5. E = **-2**

Use <, >, or = for each ○.

1. -8 ○ 8   2. 0 ○ -3
3. 15 ○ -16   4. ⁻4 ○ 4
5. -12 ○ -20 6. -3 ○ ⁻4

Read the following paragraph and answer the questions.

Kangaroos are furry, hopping mammals that live only in Australia. Antelope kangaroos live on the plains in the north. Gray kangaroos live mostly in the grasslands and forests of eastern and southern Australia. Red kangaroos make their home in the deserts and dry grasslands in the central part of the country, and most wallaroos live in dry, rocky hills.

1. What is the main idea of this paragraph?
Where kangaroos live in Australia.
Answers will vary.

2. List some of the important details of the paragraph.
Kangaroos are furry, hopping mammals. There are several kinds of kangaroos and they live in different places. (Child could list the kinds of kangaroos and where they are found.)

Page 8

What products might we get from the seven major regions of our country? See if you can put the correct region next to the correct products.

• Great Lakes • Mountain   • Southwest   • Northeast
• Plains   • Pacific   • Southeast

Southeast 1. The main crops are sugarcane, oranges, soybeans, rice, peanuts, and tobacco. The main minerals are oil, iron ore, limestone, and coal. Hickory, oak, maple, and lots of other trees are used for furniture, paper, and other products.

Northeast 2. Fish and shellfish are found here: cod, butterfish, clams, lobsters, squid, sea bass, flounder, sole, and swordfish. Farm products include milk, cheese, eggs, fruits, vegetables, chickens, turkeys, tomatoes, blueberries, cranberries, maple syrup, and grapes. This region also produces lots of coal.

Plains 3. Record amounts of corn, soybeans, and oats are found here. Other crops include fruits and vegetables. This area is rich in minerals, iron ore, and coal. This area is also rich in dairy products. This is called the "Corn Belt" of the United States.

Great Lakes 4. Corn and wheat grow well here. A lot of farming, ranching, and mining is done here. Manufacturers produce hot dogs, flour, and breakfast cereals.

Southwest 5. The largest crop in this area is cotton. Other crops are oranges, grapefruit, rice, and wheat. They raise lots of cattle and sheep here. Silver and copper are found in this region. Fuels are also plentiful, such as coal, natural gas, and oil.

Pacific 6. A wide variety of products come from here because of the two very different climate areas. Products include oil, king crab, salmon, and timber, as well as pineapple, macadamia nuts, fruits, nuts, berries, and vegetables. This area also produces petroleum and natural gas. It has the top agricultural state in the nation, as well as the top commercial fishing region.

Mountain 7. Some of the major minerals found in this region are gold, lead, silver, copper, and zinc. There is also lots of natural gas, coal, and oil to be found. Wheat, peas, beans, sugar beets, and potatoes are grown here. Ranching includes beef cattle, sheep, and dairy cows.

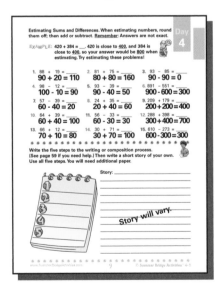

Page 9

Estimating Sums and Differences. When estimating numbers, round them off; then add or subtract. Remember: Answers are not exact.

EXAMPLE: 420 + 384 = . 420 is close to 400, and 384 is close to 400, so your answer would be 800 when estimating. Try estimating these problems!

1. 88 + 19 = 90 + 20 = **110**   2. 81 + 75 = 80 + 80 = **160**   3. 93 − 85 = 90 − 90 = **0**
4. 98 − 12 = 100 − 10 = **90**   5. 93 − 39 = 90 − 40 = **50**   6. 891 − 551 = 900 − 600 = **300**
7. 57 − 39 = 60 − 40 = **20**   8. 24 + 45 = 20 + 40 = **60**   9. 209 + 179 = 200 + 200 = **400**
10. 64 + 39 = 60 + 40 = **100**   11. 56 − 33 = 60 − 30 = **30**   12. 288 + 398 = 300 + 400 = **700**
13. 66 + 12 = 70 + 10 = **80**   14. 30 + 71 = 30 + 70 = **100** 15. 610 − 273 = 600 − 300 = **300**

Write the five steps to the writing or composition process. (See page 59 if you need help.) Then write a short story of your own. Use all five steps. You will need additional paper.

Story:
Story will vary.

Page 10

Prefixes are syllables added to the beginning of a base word. Add a prefix to these base words.

1. Will you **un**lock the door?
2. Can you **re**call what he said?
3. The genie will **dis/re**appear if you clap your hands.
4. Janet will **un/re**fold the napkins.
5. Do you **dis**agree with what I said?
6. Mother is going to **re**arrange the front room.
7. The picture was the shape of a **tri**angle.
8. Everyone needs to come **a**board now.
9. Erin and Eli will wear **uni**forms to the game.
10. You can count on me to **re**pay you.
11. Look out for the **on**coming traffic!
12. The Damons have six **tele**phones in their house.

FACTOID
Every time you lick a stamp, you're consuming 1/10 of a calorie.

A metaphor compares two different things. Here are a few metaphors written by students:
Homework is a sweaty sock: it stinks!
People are mirrors; you can see yourself in them.
Sleep is a stone, quiet and still.

Write your own metaphors by comparing two different things.

1. Sleep is
2. Life is
3. Anger is
4. Happiness is
5. Friendship is
Answers will vary.

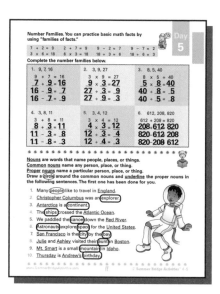

Page 11

Number Families. You can practice basic math facts by using "families of facts."

7 + 2 = 9	7 = 9 − 2	9 − 2 = 7	9 − 7 = 2
2 + 7 = 9	18 = 3 × 6	3 × 6 = 18	18 ÷ 6 = 3
3 × 6 = 18	6 × 3 = 18	18 ÷ 3 = 6	18 ÷ 6 = 3

Complete the number families below.

1. 9, 7, 16
7 + 9 = 16
9 + 7 = 16
16 − 9 = 7
16 − 7 = 9

2. 3, 9, 27
3 × 9 = 27
9 × 3 = 27
27 ÷ 9 = 3
27 ÷ 3 = 9

3. 8, 5, 40
8 × 5 = 40
5 × 8 = 40
40 ÷ 8 = 5
40 ÷ 5 = 8

4. 3, 8, 11
8 + 3 = 11
3 + 8 = 11
11 − 3 = 8
11 − 8 = 3

5. 3, 4, 12
3 × 4 = 12
4 × 3 = 12
12 ÷ 3 = 4
12 ÷ 4 = 3

6. 612, 208, 820
208 + 612 = 820
612 + 208 = 820
820 − 208 = 612
820 − 612 = 208

Nouns are words that name people, places, or things.
Common nouns name any person, place, or thing.
Proper nouns name a particular person, place, or thing.
Draw a circle around the common nouns and underline the proper nouns in the following sentences. The first one has been done for you.

1. Many people like to travel in England.
2. Christopher Columbus was an explorer.
3. Antarctica is a continent.
4. The ships crossed the Atlantic Ocean.
5. We paddled the canoe down the Red River.
6. Astronauts explore space for the United States.
7. San Francisco is the city by the bay.
8. Julie and Ashley visited their aunt in Boston.
9. Mt. Smart is a small mountain in Idaho.
10. Thursday is Andrew's birthday.

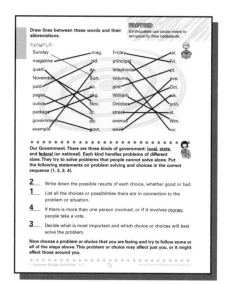

Page 12

Draw lines between these words and their abbreviations.

FACTOID Earthquakes can cause rivers to temporarily flow backwards.

EXAMPLE:

Sunday		mag.	Friday		tel.
magazine		Mar.	principal		Fri.
quart		ex.	telephone		pt.
November		Sun.	volume		ave.
paid		pd.	pint		Oct.
pages		pkg.	William		wk.
ounce		Nov.	October		prin.
package		oz.	street		Wm.
government		pp.	avenue		st.
example		govt.	week		vol.

Our Government. There are three kinds of government: local, state, and federal (or national). Each kind handles problems of different sizes. They try to solve problems that people cannot solve alone. Put the following statements on problem solving and choices in the correct sequence (1, 2, 3, 4).

2 Write down the possible results of each choice, whether good or bad.

1 List all the choices or possibilities there are in connection to the problem or situation.

4 If there is more than one person involved, or if it involves money, people take a vote.

3 Decide what is most important and which choice or choices will best solve the problem.

Now choose a problem or choice that you are facing and try to follow some or all of the steps above. This problem or choice may affect just you, or it might affect those around you.

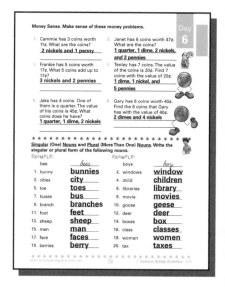

Page 13

Money Sense. Make sense of these money problems.

1. Cammie has 3 coins worth 11¢. What are the coins?
2 nickels and 1 penny

2. Janet has 6 coins worth 47¢. What are the coins?
1 quarter, 1 dime, 2 nickels, and 2 pennies

3. Frankie has 5 coins worth 17¢. What 5 coins add up to 17¢?
3 nickels and 2 pennies

4. Tenley has 7 coins. The value of the coins is 45¢. Find 7 coins with the value of 20¢.
1 dime, 1 nickel, and 5 pennies

5. Jake has 4 coins. One of them is a quarter. The value of his coins is 45¢. What coins does he have?
1 quarter, 1 dime, 2 nickels

6. Gary has 6 coins worth 40¢. Find the 6 coins that Gary has with the value of 40¢.
2 dimes and 4 nickels

Singular (One) Nouns and Plural (More Than One) Nouns. Write the singular or plural form of the following nouns.

EXAMPLE: bee — bees   EXAMPLE: boys — boy

1. bunny — **bunnies**
3. cities — **city**
5. toe — **toes**
7. buses — **bus**
9. branch — **branches**
11. foot — **feet**
13. sheep — **sheep**
15. men — **man**
17. face — **faces**
19. berries — **berry**

2. windows — **window**
4. child — **children**
6. libraries — **library**
8. movie — **movies**
10. goose — **geese**
12. deer — **deer**
14. boxes — **box**
16. class — **classes**
18. woman — **women**
20. tax — **taxes**

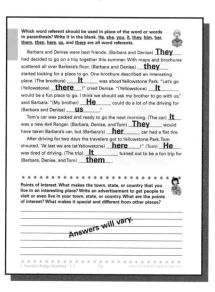

Page 14

Which word referent should be used in place of the word or words in parentheses? Write it in the blank. He, she, you, it, they, him, her, them, then, here, us, and there are all word referents.

Barbara and Denise were best friends. (Barbara and Denise) **They** had decided to go on a trip together this summer. With maps and brochures scattered all over Barbara's floor, (Barbara and Denise) **they** started looking for a place to go. One brochure described an interesting place. (The brochure) **It** was about Yellowstone Park. "Let's go (Yellowstone) **there** !" cried Denise. "(Yellowstone) **It** would be a fun place to go. I think we should ask my brother to go with us," said Barbara. "(My brother) **He** could do a lot of the driving for (Barbara and Denise) **us** ."

Tom's car was packed and ready to go the next morning. (The car) **It** was a new 4x4 Ranger. (Barbara, Denise, and Tom) **They** would have taken Barbara's car, but (Barbara's) **her** car had a flat tire.

After driving for two days the travelers got to Yellowstone Park. Tom shouted, "At last we are (at Yellowstone) **here** !" (Tom) **He** was tired of driving. (The trip) **It** turned out to be a fun trip for (Barbara, Denise, and Tom) **them** .

Points of Interest. What makes the town, state, or country that you live in an interesting place? Write an advertisement to get people to visit or even live in your town, state, or country. What are the points of interest? What makes it special and different from other places?

Answers will vary.

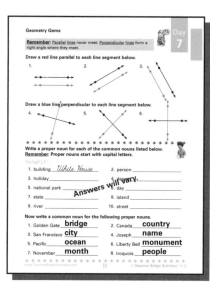

Page 15

Geometry Gems

Remember: Parallel lines never meet. Perpendicular lines form a right angle where they meet.

Draw a red line parallel to each line segment below.

Draw a blue line perpendicular to each line segment below.

Write a proper noun for each of the common nouns listed below.
Remember: Proper nouns start with capital letters.

EXAMPLE:
1. building — *White House*
2. person — _____
3. holiday — _____
4. day — _____
5. national park — _____
6. island — _____
7. state — _____
8. island — _____
9. river — _____
10. street — _____

Answers will vary.

Now write a common noun for the following proper nouns.

1. Golden Gate — **bridge**
2. Canada — **country**
3. San Francisco — **city**
4. Joseph — **name**
5. Pacific — **ocean**
6. Liberty Bell — **monument**
7. November — **month**
8. Iroquois — **people**

Page 16

Father's Day. Write about fathers; then draw a picture. Fathers should always... Fathers should never... If I were a father I would want to always...

Answers will vary.

Draw your picture here!

Pictures will vary.

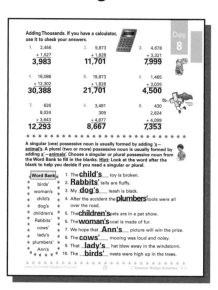

Page 17

Adding Thousands. If you have a calculator, use it to check your answers.

1. 2,456 + 1,527 = **3,983**
2. 9,873 + 1,828 = **11,701**
3. 4,678 + 3,321 = **7,999**
4. 18,086 + 12,302 = **30,388**
5. 19,873 + 1,828 = **21,701**
6. 1,465 + 3,035 = **4,500**
7. 626 + 8,024 + 3,643 = **12,293**
8. 3,481 + 309 + 4,877 = **8,667**
9. 430 + 2,824 + 4,099 = **7,353**

A singular (one) possessive noun is usually formed by adding 's—*animals*. A plural (two or more) possessive noun is usually formed by adding s—*animals'*. Choose a singular or plural possessive noun from the Word Bank to fill in the blanks. **Hint:** Look at the word after the blank to help you decide if you need a singular or plural.

Word Bank: birds', woman's, child's, dog's, children's, Rabbits', cows', lady's, plumbers', Ann's

1. The **child's** toy is broken.
2. **Rabbits'** tails are fluffy.
3. My **dog's** leash is black.
4. After the accident the **plumbers'** tools were all over the road.
5. The **children's** pets are in a pet show.
6. The **woman's** coat is made of fur.
7. We hope that **Ann's** picture will win the prize.
8. The **cows'** mooing was loud and noisy.
9. That **lady's** hat blew away in the windstorm.
10. The **birds'** nests were high up in the trees.

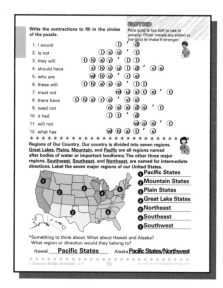

Page 18

Write the contractions to fill in the circles of the puzzle.

FACTOID Pure gold is too soft to use in jewelry. Other metals are added to the gold to make it stronger.

1. I would — I'd
2. is not — isn't
3. they will — they'll
4. should have — should've
5. who are — who're
6. these will — these'll
7. must not — mustn't
8. there have — there've
9. need not — needn't
10. it had — it'd
11. will not — won't
12. what has — what's

Regions of Our Country. Our country is divided into seven regions. Great Lakes, Plains, Mountain, and Pacific are all regions named after bodies of water or important landforms. The other three major regions, Southwest, Southeast, and Northeast, are named for intermediate directions. Label the seven major regions of our United States.

1. **Pacific States**
2. **Mountain States**
3. **Plain States**
4. **Great Lake States**
5. **Northeast**
6. **Southeast**
7. **Southwest**

*Something to think about. What about Hawaii and Alaska? What region or direction would they belong to?

Hawaii **Pacific States**   Alaska **Pacific States/Northwest**

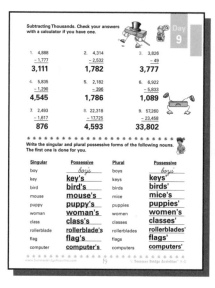

Page 19

Subtracting Thousands. Check your answers with a calculator if you have one.

1. 4,888 − 1,777 = **3,111**
2. 4,314 − 2,532 = **1,782**
3. 3,826 − 49 = **3,777**
4. 5,835 − 1,290 = **4,545**
5. 2,182 − 396 = **1,786**
6. 6,922 − 5,833 = **1,089**
7. 2,493 − 1,617 = **876**
8. 22,318 − 17,725 = **4,593**
9. 57,260 − 23,458 = **33,802**

Write the singular and plural possessive forms of the following nouns. The first one is done for you.

Singular	Possessive	Plural	Possessive
boy	*boy's*	boys	*boys'*
key	**key's**	keys	**keys'**
bird	**bird's**	birds	**birds'**
mouse	**mouse's**	mice	**mice's**
puppy	**puppy's**	puppies	**puppies'**
woman	**woman's**	women	**women's**
class	**class's**	classes	**classes'**
rollerblade	**rollerblade's**	rollerblades	**rollerblades'**
flag	**flag's**	flags	**flags'**
computer	**computer's**	computers	**computers'**

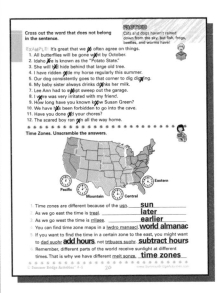

Cross out the word that does not belong in the sentence.

FACTOID Cats and dogs haven't rained down from the sky, but fish, frogs, beetles, and worms have!

EXAMPLE: It's great that we ~~all~~ often agree on things.
1. All butterflies will be gone ~~went~~ by October.
2. Idaho ~~are~~ is known as the "Potato State."
3. She will ~~hid~~ hide behind that large old tree.
4. I have ridden ~~rode~~ my horse regularly this summer.
5. Our dog consistently goes to that corner to dig ~~digging~~.
6. My baby sister always drinks ~~drinks~~ her milk.
7. Lee Ann had to ~~swept~~ sweep out the garage.
8. I ~~were~~ was very irritated with my friend.
9. How long have you known ~~know~~ Susan Green?
10. We have ~~his~~ been forbidden to go into the cave.
11. Have you done ~~did~~ your chores?
12. The scared boy ran ~~run~~ all the way home.

Time Zones. Unscramble the answers.

1. Time zones are different because of the usn. **sun**
2. As we go east the time is treal. **later**
3. As we go west the time is rrilaee. **earlier**
4. You can find time zone maps in a lwdro manaaci. **world almanac**
5. If you want to find the time in a certain zone to the east, you might want to dad suohr **add hours**, not trtbuacs suohr. **subtract hours**
6. Remember, different parts of the world receive sunlight at different times. That is why we have different meit sonze. **time zones**

Page 20

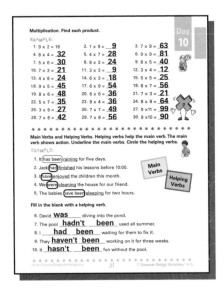

Multiplication. Find each product.

EXAMPLE:
1. 9 x 2 = 18
2. 1 x 9 = __9__
3. 7 x 9 = __63__
4. 8 x 4 = __32__
5. 4 x 7 = __28__
6. 9 x 9 = __81__
7. 5 x 6 = __30__
8. 8 x 3 = __24__
9. 8 x 5 = __40__
10. 7 x 3 = __21__
11. 3 x 3 = __9__
12. 3 x 4 = __12__
13. 4 x 6 = __24__
14. 6 x 3 = __18__
15. 5 x 5 = __25__
16. 9 x 5 = __45__
17. 9 x 6 = __54__
18. 8 x 7 = __56__
19. 8 x 6 = __48__
20. 6 x 6 = __36__
21. 7 x 3 = __21__
22. 5 x 7 = __35__
23. 4 x 9 = __36__
24. 8 x 8 = __64__
25. 3 x 9 = __27__
26. 7 x 7 = __49__
27. 9 x 11 = __99__
28. 7 x 6 = __42__
29. 7 x 8 = __56__
30. 9 x 10 = __90__

Main Verbs and Helping Verbs. Helping verbs help the main verb. The main verb shows action. Underline the main verbs. Circle the helping verbs.

EXAMPLE:
1. It (has been) raining for five days.
2. Jack (had) finished his lessons before 10:00.
3. I (have) enjoyed the children this month.
4. We (were) cleaning the house for our friend.
5. The babies (have been) sleeping for two hours.

Main Verbs **Helping Verbs**

Fill in the blank with a helping verb.
6. David __was__ diving into the pond.
7. The pool __hadn't__ __been__ used all summer.
8. I __had__ __been__ waiting for them to fix it.
9. They __haven't__ __been__ working on it for three weeks.
10. It __hasn't__ __been__ fun without the pool.

Page 21

Calendar. The months of the year and the days of the week are written below in order. On the lines below write the months and days in alphabetical order. Write in cursive.

January February March April May June July August September October November December
Sunday Monday Tuesday Wednesday Thursday Friday Saturday

1. April
2. August
3. December
4. February
5. Friday
6. January
7. July
8. June
9. March
10. May
11. Monday
12. November
13. October
14. Saturday
15. September
16. Sunday
17. Thursday
18. Tuesday
19. Wednesday

World Globe. Read the information given; then label the following:
1. Northern **Hemisphere**
2. Western **Hemisphere**
3. Line of **longitude**
4. Prime **Meridian**
5. **Equator**
6. Eastern **Hemisphere**
7. Line of **latitude**
8. Southern **Hemisphere**

We use different terms to locate places on maps and globes. We use lines of latitude to go around the globe from east to west. These lines run parallel to each other, never touching each other. Lines of longitude run north and south on a map or globe and are sometimes called meridians.

The equator is a line of latitude running west to east that divides the earth in half. The top half is called the Northern Hemisphere; the bottom half is called the Southern Hemisphere. The prime meridian is a line of longitude. It runs from north to south. All longitudes are determined based on the prime meridian.

Page 22

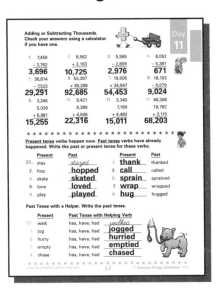

Adding or Subtracting Thousands. Check your answers using a calculator if you have one.

1. 7,458 − 3,762 = **3,696**
2. 8,562 + 2,163 = **10,725**
3. 5,585 − 2,609 = **2,976**
4. 6,052 − 5,381 = **671**
5. 36,814 − 7,523 = **29,291**
6. 53,397 + 39,288 = **92,685**
7. 19,506 + 34,947 = **54,453**
8. 18,103 − 9,079 = **9,024**
9. 3,245 + 5,029 + 6,981 = **15,255**
10. 9,421 + 8,389 + 4,506 = **22,316**
11. 3,340 + 7,189 + 4,482 = **15,011**
12. 46,306 + 18,782 + 3,115 = **68,203**

Present tense verbs happen now. Past tense verbs have already happened. Write the past or present tense for these verbs.

Present	Past		Present	Past
EX. stay	stayed			
2. hop	**hopped**	3. **thank**	thanked
4. skate	**skated**	5. call	called
6. love	**loved**	7. **sprain**	sprained
8. play	**played**	9. **wrap**	wrapped
		11. **hug**	hugged

Past Tense with a Helper. Write the past tense.

Present	Past Tense with Helping Verb
EX. walk	has, have, had	walked
1. jog	has, have, had	**jogged**
2. hurry	has, have, had	**hurried**
3. empty	has, have, had	**emptied**
4. chase	has, have, had	**chased**

Page 23

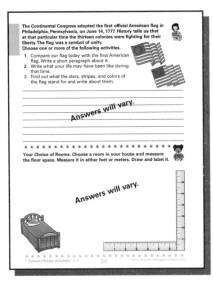

The Continental Congress adopted the first official American flag in Philadelphia, Pennsylvania, on June 14, 1777. History tells us that at that particular time the thirteen colonies were fighting for their liberty. The flag was a symbol of unity. Choose one or more of the following activities.

1. Compare our flag today with the first American flag. Write a short paragraph about it.
2. Write what your life may have been like during that time.
3. Find out what the stars, stripes, and colors of the flag stand for and write about them.

Answers will vary.

Your Choice of Rooms. Choose a room in your house and measure the floor space. Measure it in either feet or meters. Draw and label it.

Answers will vary.

Page 24

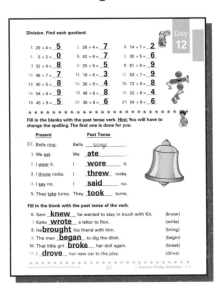

Division. Find each quotient.
1. 20 ÷ 4 = **5**
2. 28 ÷ 4 = **7**
3. 14 ÷ 7 = **2**
4. 0 ÷ 2 = **0**
5. 42 ÷ 6 = **7**
6. 30 ÷ 5 = **6**
7. 32 ÷ 4 = **8**
8. 25 ÷ 5 = **5**
9. 81 ÷ 9 = **9**
10. 49 ÷ 7 = **7**
11. 18 ÷ 6 = **3**
12. 63 ÷ 7 = **9**
13. 40 ÷ 5 = **8**
14. 36 ÷ 9 = **4**
15. 72 ÷ 9 = **8**
16. 54 ÷ 6 = **9**
17. 48 ÷ 6 = **8**
18. 32 ÷ 8 = **4**
19. 45 ÷ 9 = **5**
20. 36 ÷ 6 = **6**
21. 54 ÷ 9 = **6**

Fill in the blanks with the past tense verb. Hint: You will have to change the spelling. The first one is done for you.

Present	Past Tense
EX. Bells ring.	Bells __rang__.
1. We eat.	We __ate__.
2. I wear it.	I __wore__ it.
3. I throw rocks.	I __threw__ rocks.
4. I say no.	I __said__ no.
5. They take turns.	They __took__ turns.

Fill in the blank with the past tense of the verb.
6. Sam __knew__ he wanted to stay in touch with Kit. (know)
7. Katie __wrote__ a letter to Ron. (write)
8. He __brought__ his friend with him. (bring)
9. The men __began__ to dig the ditch. (begin)
10. That little girl __broke__ her doll again. (break)
11. I __drove__ her new car to the play. (drive)

Page 25

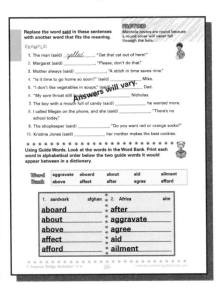

Replace the word said in these sentences with another word that fits the meaning.

FACTOID Manhole covers are round because a round cover will never fall through the hole.

EXAMPLE:
1. The man (said) __yelled__, "Get that cat out of here!"
2. Margaret (said) _____, "Please, don't do that."
3. Mother always (said) _____, "A stitch in time saves nine."
4. "Is it time to go home so soon?" (said) _____ Mike.
5. "I don't like vegetables in soups," (said) _____ Dad.
6. "My sore throat still _____" Nicholas.
7. The boy with a mouth full of candy (said) _____ he wanted more.
8. I called Megan on the phone, and she (said) _____, "There's no school today."
9. The shopkeeper (said) _____, "Do you want red or orange socks?"
10. Kristine Jones (said) _____ her mother makes the best cookies.

Answers will vary.

Using Guide Words. Look at the words in the Word Bank. Print each word in alphabetical order below the two guide words it would appear between in a dictionary.

Word Bank				
aggravate	aboard	about	aid	ailment
above	affect	after	agree	afford

1. aardvark — afghan	2. Africa — aim
aboard	**after**
about	**aggravate**
above	**agree**
affect	**aid**
afford	**ailment**

Page 26

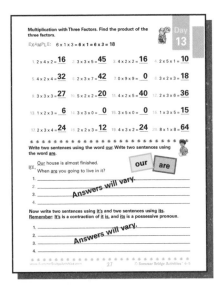

Multiplication with Three Factors. Find the product of the three factors.

EXAMPLE: 6 x 1 x 3 = 6 x 1 = 6 x 3 = 18

1. 2 x 4 x 2 = **16**
2. 3 x 3 x 5 = **45**
3. 4 x 2 x 2 = **16**
4. 2 x 5 x 1 = **10**
5. 4 x 2 x 4 = **32**
6. 2 x 3 x 7 = **42**
7. 0 x 9 x 9 = **0**
8. 3 x 2 x 3 = **18**
9. 3 x 3 x 3 = **27**
10. 5 x 2 x 2 = **20**
11. 4 x 2 x 5 = **40**
12. 2 x 3 x 6 = **36**
13. 1 x 2 x 3 = **6**
14. 3 x 3 x 0 = **0**
15. 3 x 5 x 0 = **0**
16. 1 x 3 x 5 = **15**
17. 2 x 3 x 4 = **24**
18. 2 x 2 x 3 = **12**
19. 4 x 2 x 2 = **24**
20. 8 x 1 x 8 = **64**

Write two sentences using the word our. Write two sentences using the word are.

EX. Our house is almost finished.
When are you going to live in it?

our **are**

1. _____
2. _____
3. _____
4. _____
Answers will vary.

Now write two sentences using it's and two sentences using its.
Remember: It's is a contraction of it is, and its is a possessive pronoun.

1. _____
2. _____
3. _____
4. _____
Answers will vary.

Page 27

FACTOID Penguins have a special organ near their eyes that can change salt water into fresh water.

A Trip to Outer Space. We're planning a big trip into outer space! You are invited to come along, too. You can even invite a few friends. What will you pack? Why? Where shall we go? What needs to be done? What do you think will happen? What will it be like? Think, then write!

Answers will vary.

Page 28

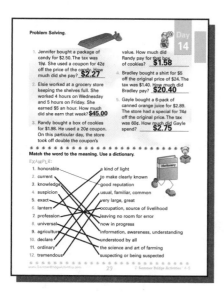

Page 29

Problem Solving.

1. Jennifer bought a package of candy for $2.50. The tax was 19¢. She used a coupon for 42¢ off the price of the candy. How much did she pay? **$2.27**

2. Elsie worked at a grocery store keeping the shelves full. She worked 4 hours on Wednesday and 5 hours on Friday. She earned $5 an hour. How much did she earn that week? **$45.00**

3. Randy bought a box of cookies for $1.98. He used a 20¢ coupon. On this particular day, the store took off double the coupon's value. How much did Randy pay for that box of cookies? **$1.58**

4. Bradley bought a shirt for $5 off the original price of $24. The tax was $1.40. How much did Bradley pay? **$20.40**

5. Gayle bought a 6-pack of canned orange juice for $2.89. The store had a special for 74¢ off the original price. The tax was 60¢. How much did Gayle spend? **$2.75**

Match the word to the meaning. Use a dictionary.

1. honorable — good reputation
2. current — now in progress
3. knowledge — information, awareness, understanding
4. suspicion — suspecting or being suspected
5. exact — leaving no room for error
6. lantern — a kind of light
7. profession — occupation, source of livelihood
8. universal — understood by all
9. agriculture — the science and art of farming
10. declare — to make clearly known
11. ordinary — usual, familiar, common
12. tremendous — very large, great

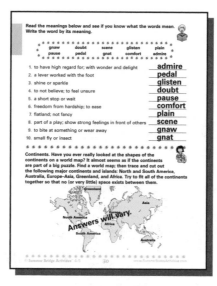

Page 30

Read the meanings below and see if you know what the words mean. Write the word by its meaning.

gnaw, doubt, scene, glisten, plain, pause, pedal, gnat, comfort, admire

1. to have high regard for; with wonder and delight — **admire**
2. a lever worked with the foot — **pedal**
3. shine or sparkle — **glisten**
4. to not believe; to feel unsure — **doubt**
5. a short stop or wait — **pause**
6. freedom from hardship; to ease — **comfort**
7. flatland; not fancy — **plain**
8. part of a play; show strong feelings in front of others — **scene**
9. to bite at something or wear away — **gnaw**
10. small fly or insect — **gnat**

Continents. Have you ever really looked at the shapes of the continents on a world map? It almost seems as if the continents are part of a big puzzle. Find a world map; then trace and cut out the following major continents and islands: North and South America, Australia, Europe–Asia, Greenland, and Africa. Try to fit all of the continents together so that no (or very little) space exists between them.

Answers will vary.

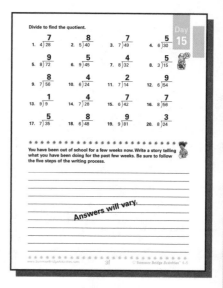

Page 31

Divide to find the quotient.

1. 4)28 = 7	2. 5)40 = 8	3. 7)49 = 7	4. 6)30 = 5
5. 8)72 = 9	6. 9)45 = 5	7. 8)32 = 4	8. 3)15 = 5
9. 7)56 = 8	10. 6)24 = 4	11. 7)14 = 2	12. 6)54 = 9
13. 9)9 = 1	14. 7)28 = 4	15. 6)42 = 7	16. 8)56 = 7
17. 7)35 = 5	18. 6)48 = 8	19. 9)81 = 9	20. 8)24 = 3

You have been out of school for a few weeks now. Write a story telling what you have been doing for the past few weeks. Be sure to follow the five steps of the writing process.

Answers will vary.

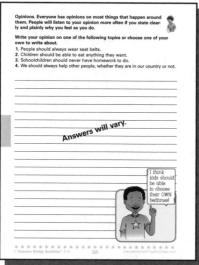

Page 32

Below are the days of the week and the months of the year spelled with dictionary symbols. Write the words to the side. Don't forget capital letters.

FACTOID Oats are sometimes used as a preservative in ice cream.

1. /ā′prəl/ — April
2. /märch/ — March
3. /jan′ū er′ē/ — January
4. /wenz′dā/ — Wednesday
5. /mun′dā/ — Monday
6. /jūn/ — June
7. /sep′tem′bər/ — September
8. /sun′dā/ — Sunday
9. /dē sem′bər/ — December
10. /nō vem′bər/ — November
11. /sat′ər dā/ — Saturday
12. /ô′gest/ — August
13. /mā/ — May
14. /thərz′dā/ — Thursday
15. /feb′rūer′ē/ — February
16. /ok tō′bər/ — October
17. /tūz′dā/ — Tuesday
18. /jūlī′/ — July
19. /frī′dā/ — Friday

Chord—a line segment passing through a circle that has its endpoints on that circle
Circumference—the distance around a circle
Diameter—a chord passing through the center of a circle
Radius—a line segment with one endpoint at the center of a circle and the other endpoint on the circle

Draw an example for each term.

Draw a radius AB. | Draw a diameter XY. | Trace the circumference. | Draw a chord DE.

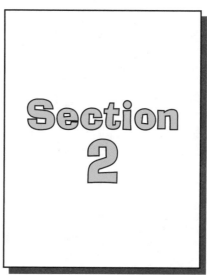

Section 2

Page 37

Write the rest of the number families.

1. 6 × 9 = 54 / 9 × 6 = 54 / 54 ÷ 6 = 9 / 54 ÷ 9 = 6
2. 8 × 7 = 56 / 7 × 8 = 56 / 56 ÷ 6 = 8 / 56 ÷ 7 = 8
3. 6 × 7 = 42 / 7 × 6 = 42 / 42 ÷ 6 = 7 / 42 ÷ 7 = 6
4. 48 ÷ 8 = 6 / 48 ÷ 6 = 8 / 6 × 8 = 48 / 8 × 6 = 48
5. 72 ÷ 8 = 9 / 72 ÷ 9 = 8 / 9 × 8 = 72 / 8 × 9 = 72
6. 6 × 9 = 54 / 9 × 6 = 54 / 54 ÷ 9 = 6 / 54 ÷ 6 = 9
7. 36 ÷ 4 = 9 / 36 ÷ 9 = 4 / 4 × 9 = 36 / 9 × 4 = 36
8. 9 × 7 = 63 / 7 × 9 = 63 / 63 ÷ 9 = 7 / 63 ÷ 7 = 9
9. 5 × 9 = 45 / 9 × 5 = 45 / 45 ÷ 9 = 5 / 45 ÷ 5 = 9

Prefixes and Suffixes. Remember: Prefixes are added to the beginning of a base word. Suffixes are added to the end of a base word. Add a prefix to these words. Use mis-, un-, and re-. Write the whole word.

mis- un- re-

1. lucky — **unlucky**
2. judge — **misjudge**
3. spell — **misspell**
4. fill — **refill**
5. build — **rebuild**
6. able — **unable**

Add a suffix to these words. Use -er, -less, -ful, and -ed. Write the whole word.

7. use — **useful, useless**
8. spell — **spelled, speller**
9. care — **careful, careless**
10. hope — **hopeful, hopeless, hoped**
11. sing — **singer**
12. teach — **teacher**

Now write two sentences using words of your choice from each of the two word lists above.

1. _____
2. _____

Sentences will vary.

Page 38

Opinions. Everyone has opinions on most things that happen around them. People will listen to your opinion more often if you state clearly and plainly why you feel as you do.

Write your opinion on one of the following topics or choose one of your own to write about.

1. People should always wear seat belts.
2. Children should be able to eat anything they want.
3. Schoolchildren should never have homework to do.
4. We should always help other people, whether they are in our country or not.

Answers will vary.

I think kids should be able to choose their OWN bedtime!

Page 39

Find the product by multiplying.

EXAMPLE: 12 × 6 = 72

1. 12 × 4 = 48	2. 22 × 6 = 132	3. 18 × 2 = 36	4. 23 × 4 = 92
5. 23 × 7 = 161	6. 34 × 6 = 204	7. 16 × 5 = 80	8. 78 × 5 = 390
9. 86 × 7 = 602	10. 69 × 9 = 621	11. 57 × 4 = 228	12. 62 × 6 = 372	13. 97 × 7 = 679

Think of your five senses to help you describe the words below. Try to come up with a word for each sense.

EXAMPLE:

	taste	touch	smell	sight	sound
fire	smoky	hot	smoky	bright	crackle
candy bar	sweet	smooth	chocolate	brown	crunchy

1. a red rose _____
2. a rainbow _____
3. a barnyard _____
4. a snake's skin _____
5. a snowflake _____

Sentences will vary.

Choose one of the above and write a paragraph about it. Be very descriptive and put in a lot of details.

Paragraphs will vary.

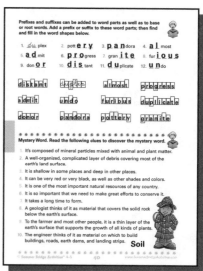

Page 40

Prefixes and suffixes can be added to word parts as well as to base or root words. Add a prefix or suffix to these word parts; then find and fill in the word shapes below.

1. dī plex
2. pott **ery**
3. **pan** dora
4. **al** most
5. **ad** mit
6. **pro** gress
7. gran **ite**
8. fur **ious**
9. don **or**
10. **dis** tant
11. **du** plicate
12. **un** do

distant | dogtag | almost | progress
admit | undo | furious | duplicate
donor | pandora | pottery | granite

Mystery Word. Read the following clues to discover the mystery word.

1. It's composed of mineral particles mixed with animal and plant matter.
2. A well-organized, complicated layer of debris covering most of the earth's land surface.
3. It is shallow in some places and deep in other places.
4. It can be very red or very black, as well as other shades and colors.
5. It is one of the most important natural resources of any country.
6. It is so important that we need to make great efforts to conserve it.
7. It takes a long time to form.
8. A geologist thinks of it as material that covers the solid rock below the earth's surface.
9. To the farmer and most other people, it is a thin layer of the earth's surface that supports the growth of all kinds of plants.
10. The engineer thinks of it as material on which to build buildings, roads, earth dams, and landing strips. **Soil**

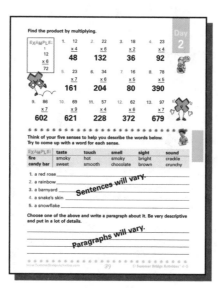

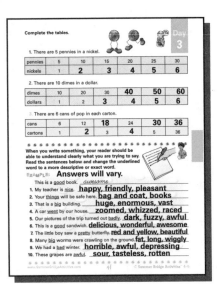

Complete the tables.

Day 3

1. There are 5 pennies in a nickel.

pennies	5	10	15	20	25	30
nickels	1	2	3	4	5	6

2. There are 10 dimes in a dollar.

dimes	10	20	30	40	50	60
dollars	1	2	3	4	5	6

3. There are 6 cans of pop in each carton.

cans	6	12	18	24	30	36
cartons	1	2	3	4	5	36

When you write something, your reader should be able to understand clearly what you are trying to say. Read the sentences below and change the underlined word to a more descriptive or exact word.

EXAMPLE: **Answers will vary.**

This is a good book. *awesome*

1. My teacher is nice. **happy, friendly, pleasant**
2. Your things will be safe here. **bag and coat, books**
3. That is a big building. **huge, enormous, vast**
4. A car went by our house. **zoomed, whizzed, raced**
5. Our pictures of the trip turned out badly. **dark, fuzzy, awful**
6. This is a good sandwich. **delicious, wonderful, awesome**
7. The little boy saw a pretty butterfly. **red and yellow, beautiful**
8. Many big worms were crawling on the ground. **fat, long, wiggly**
9. We had a bad winter. **horrible, awful, depressing**
10. These grapes are awful. **sour, tasteless, rotten**

www.SummerBridgeActivities.com 41 © Summer Bridge Activities™ 4-5

Page 41

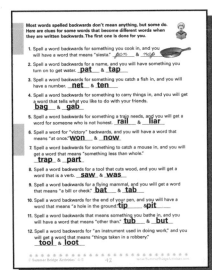

Most words spelled backwards don't mean anything, but some do. Here are clues for some words that become different words when they are written backwards. The first one is done for you.

1. Spell a word backwards for something you cook in, and you will have a word that means "siesta." *pan* & *nap*
2. Spell a word backwards for a name, and you will have something you turn on to get water. **pat** & **tap**
3. Spell a word backwards for something you catch a fish in, and you will have a number. **net** & **ten**
4. Spell a word backwards for something to carry things in, and you will get a word that tells what you like to do with your friends. **bag** & **gab**
5. Spell a word backwards for something a train needs, and you will get a word for someone who is not honest. **rail** & **liar**
6. Spell a word for "victory" backwards, and you will have a word that means "at once." **won** & **now**
7. Spell a word backwards for something to catch a mouse in, and you will get a word that means "something less than whole." **trap** & **part**
8. Spell a word backwards for a tool that cuts wood, and you will get a word that is a verb. **saw** & **was**
9. Spell a word backwards for a flying mammal, and you will get a word that means "a bill or check." **bat** & **tab**
10. Spell a word backwards for the end of your pen, and you will have a word that means "a hole in the ground." **tip** & **pit**
11. Spell a word backwards that means something you bathe in, and you will have a word that means "other than." **tub** & **but**
12. Spell a word backwards for "an instrument used in doing work," and you will get a word that means "things taken in a robbery." **tool** & **loot**

© Summer Bridge Activities™ 4-5 42 www.SummerBridgeActivities.com

Page 42

Your little finger is about 1 centimeter wide. If you don't have a centimeter tape, use a string and this centimeter ruler to measure for the following activities.

Day 4

1. The length of your shoes ________
2. The length and width of this book ________, ________
3. Your neck measure ________
4. Your kitchen table length and width ________, ________
5. Your height in centimeters ________
6. The width of a chair in your home ________

Answers will vary.

How many other things can you measure? Try estimating; then check to see how close you come to the exact measurement.

Answers will vary.

Underline the pronouns in the following sentences.
Remember: A pronoun takes the place of a noun.

1. Will you go with us?
2. Tomorrow we will go home.
3. He did a good job.
4. This book came for him.
5. She went with me.
6. A package came for us.
7. We ate all of them.
8. You are a good sport.
9. It is time for her to go.
10. He and I ate the apples.
11. I thanked him for it.
12. It was very good.

www.SummerBridgeActivities.com 43 © Summer Bridge Activities™ 4-5

Page 43

Personification is when a writer gives human qualities to a non-living thing. An example of this is when the flower in *Alice in Wonderland* talks to Alice. Personify (or give life to) the following things by creating a conversation between them.

What would a

1. pencil say to a hand?
2. carpet say to a foot?
3. basketball say to a basketball player?
4. skateboard say to a skateboarder?

Answers will vary.

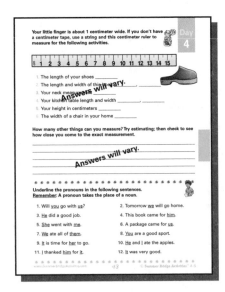

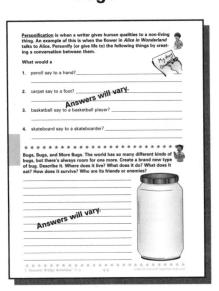

Bugs, Bugs, and More Bugs. The world has so many different kinds of bugs, but there's always room for one more. Create a brand new type of bug. Describe it. Where does it live? What does it eat? How does it survive? Who are its friends or enemies?

Answers will vary.

© Summer Bridge Activities™ 4-5 44 www.SummerBridgeActivities.com

Page 44

Multiplying with tens and hundreds is fast and fun.

Day 5

1. 4 x 10 = **40**
2. 600 x 6 = **3,600**
3. 7 x 800 = **5,600**
4. 30 x 8 = **240**
5. 5 x 20 = **100**
6. 800 x 5 = **4,000**
7. 8 x 90 = **720**
8. 50 x 6 = **300**
9. 600 x 5 = **3,000**
10. 4 x 100 = **400**
11. 7 x 80 = **560**
12. 7 x 500 = **3,500**
13. 900 x 7 = **6,300**
14. 600 x 4 = **2,400**
15. 900 x 4 = **3,600**
16. 8 x 900 = **7,200**
17. 800 x 2 = **1,600**
18. 7 x 900 = **6,300**
19. 3 x 10 = **30**
20. 700 x 6 = **4,200**
21. 3 x 800 = **2,400**
22. 7 x 40 = **280**
23. 9 x 10 = **90**
24. 10 x 100 = **1,000**
25. 4 x 60 = **240**
26. 80 x 2 = **160**
27. 500 x 4 = **2,000**
28. 7 x 700 = **4,900**
29. 30 x 8 = **240**
30. 800 x 6 = **4,800**

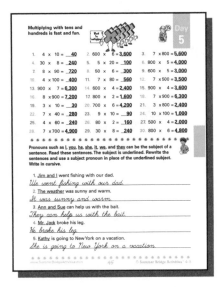

Pronouns such as I, you, he, she, it, we, and they can be the subject of a sentence. Read these sentences. The subject is underlined. Rewrite the sentences and use a subject pronoun in place of the underlined subject. Write in cursive.

1. Jim and I went fishing with our dad.
We went fishing with our dad.
2. The weather was sunny and warm.
It was sunny and warm.
3. Ann and Sue can help us with the bait.
They can help us with the bait.
4. Mr. Jack broke his leg.
He broke his leg.
5. Kathy is going to New York on a vacation.
She is going to New York on a vacation.

www.SummerBridgeActivities.com 45 © Summer Bridge Activities™ 4-5

Page 45

Categorize these words under one of the headings.
Hint: There can be eight words under each heading.
Remember: Categorizing words means to put them in groups that have something in common. One row of examples is given.

interstate	add	region	colony	bacteria	solid
oxygen	city	hemisphere	stop	column	inch
debate	larva	yield	basin	hexagon	canal
environment	speed	equal	fossil	candidate	intersection
measure	insect	bay	caution	map	estimate
numerator	freedom	society	elevation	freeway	railroad

Math Words	Geography Words	Transportation Words	Science Words	Social Studies Words
add	*region*	*interstate*	*bacteria*	*colony*
hexagon	hemisphere	caution	larva	debate
measure	bay	intersection	insect	freedom
inch	map	stop	solid	candidate
equal	basin	speed	fossil	society
numerator	canal	yield	oxygen	city
estimate	elevation	freeway		
column	environment	railroad		

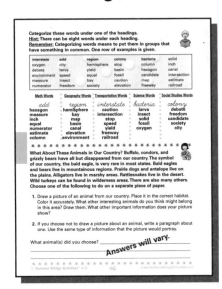

What About These Animals in Our Country? Buffalo, condors, and grizzly bears have all but disappeared from our country. The symbol of our country, the bald eagle, is very rare in most states. Bald eagles and bears live in mountainous regions. Prairie dogs and antelope live on the plains. Alligators live in marshy areas. Rattlesnakes live in the desert. Wild turkeys can be found in wilderness areas. There are also many others. Choose one of the following to do on a separate piece of paper.

1. Draw a picture of an animal from our country. Place it in the correct habitat. Color it accurately. What other interesting animals do you think might belong in this area? Draw them. What other important information does your picture show?
2. If you choose not to draw a picture about an animal, write a paragraph about one. Use the same type of information that the picture would portray.

What animal(s) did you choose? **Answers will vary.**

© Summer Bridge Activities™ 4-5 46 www.SummerBridgeActivities.com

Page 46

Addition and multiplication are related. Answer the addition problems and then write the related multiplication problem.

Day 6

EXAMPLE: 10 + 10 + 10 + 10 + 10 = 50, or 5 x 10 = 50

1. 20 + 20 + 20 = **60** — **3** x **20** = **60**
2. 9 + 9 + 9 + 9 + 9 + 9 = **54** — **6** x **9** = **54**
3. 100 + 100 + 100 + 100 = **400** — **4** x **100** = **400**
4. 8 + 8 + 8 + 8 + 8 + 8 + 8 + 8 = **64** — **8** x **8** = **64**
5. 12 + 12 + 12 + 12 = **48** — **4** x **12** = **48**
6. 75 + 75 + 75 = **225** — **3** x **75** = **225**
7. 35 + 35 + 35 + 35 + 35 + 35 = **210** — **6** x **35** = **210**
8. 51 + 51 + 51 + 51 + 51 = **255** — **5** x **51** = **255**

Use the pronouns me, her, him, it, us, you, and them after action verbs. Use I and me after the other nouns or pronouns. Circle the correct pronoun in each sentence.

1. Lily and (**I**, me) like to visit museums.
2. (**They**, Them) were very juicy oranges.
3. He helped her and (I, **me**).
4. (**We**, Us) tried not to fall as much this time.
5. Miss Green gave a shovel and bucket to (he, **him**).
6. (**I**, Me) wanted a new horse for Christmas.
7. Rick asked (she, **her**) to come with us.
8. Jason went with (they, **them**) to the mountain.
9. Mother asked (I, **me**) to fix the dinner.
10. Carla got some forks for (we, **us**).

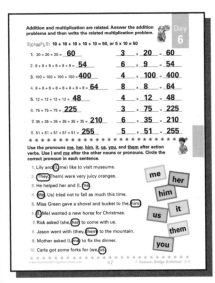

me her him it us them you

www.SummerBridgeActivities.com 47 © Summer Bridge Activities™ 4-5

Page 47

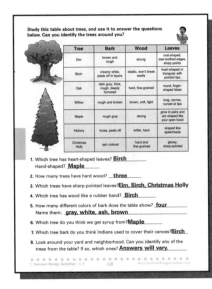

Study this table about trees, and use it to answer the questions below. Can you identify the trees around you?

Tree	Bark	Wood	Leaves
Elm	brown and rough	strong	oval-shaped, saw-toothed edges, sharp points
Birch	creamy white, peels off in layers	elastic, won't break easily	heart-shaped or triangular with pointed tips
Oak	dark gray, thick, rough, deeply furrowed	hard, fine-grained	round, finger-shaped lobes
Willow	rough and broken	brown, soft, light	long, narrow, curved at tips
Maple	rough gray	strong	grow in pairs and are shaped like your open hand
Hickory	loose, peels off	white, hard	shaped like spearheads
Christmas Holly	ash colored	hard and fine-grained	glossy, sharp-pointed

1. Which tree has heart-shaped leaves? **Birch**
Hand-shaped? **Maple**
2. How many trees have hard wood? **three**
3. Which trees have sharp-pointed leaves? **Elm, Birch, Christmas Holly**
4. Which tree has wood like a rubber band? **Birch**
5. How many different colors of bark does the table show? **four**
Name them: **gray, white, ash, brown**
6. Which tree do you think we get syrup from? **Maple**
7. Which tree bark do you think Indians used to cover their canoes? **Birch**
8. Look around your yard and neighborhood. Can you identify any of the trees from the table? If so, which ones? **Answers will vary.**

© Summer Bridge Activities™ 4-5 48 www.SummerBridgeActivities.com

Page 48

Complete this multiplication table.

Day 7

x	10	20	30	40	50	60	70	80	90
1	10	20	30	40	50	60	70	80	90
2	20	40	60	80	100	120	140	160	180
3	30	60	90	120	150	180	210	240	270
4	40	80	120	160	200	240	280	320	360
5	50	100	150	200	250	300	350	400	450
6	60	120	180	240	300	360	420	480	540
7	70	140	210	280	350	420	490	560	630
8	80	160	240	320	400	480	560	640	720
9	90	180	270	360	450	540	630	720	810

How does multiplying by hundreds differ from multiplying by tens?
Answers will vary as there is more than one way to do it.
Could you change this table to show multiplying by hundreds? **Yes**
How? **By adding a zero to each number (except for those on the left side).**

Using Its, It's, Your, and You're. It's and you're are contractions. Its and your are possessive pronouns. Fill in the blanks with it's, its, your, or you're.

1. I hope **you're** coming to my barn dance.
2. The dance will be for **your** friends also.
3. Do you think **it's** too cold for a barn dance?
4. **Its** starting time is eight o'clock.
5. Will **your** family come to the dance with you?
6. **Its** floor is long and wide.
7. **You're** coming early, aren't you?
8. I think I will need **your** help.

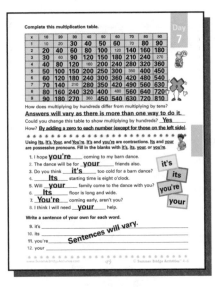

it's its you're your

Write a sentence of your own for each word.

9. it's
10. its
11. you're
12. your

Sentences will vary.

www.SummerBridgeActivities.com 49 © Summer Bridge Activities™ 4-5

Page 49

Page 50

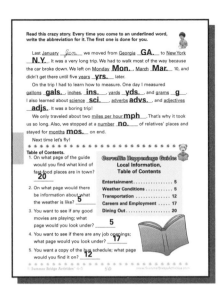

Read this crazy story. Every time you come to an underlined word, write the abbreviation for it. The first one is done for you.

Last January **Jan.** we moved from Georgia **GA.** to New York **N.Y.** It was a very long trip. We had to walk most of the way because the car broke down. We left on Monday **Mon.**, March **Mar.** 10, and didn't get there until five years **yrs.** later.

On the trip I had to learn how to measure. One day I measured gallons **gals.**, inches **ins.**, yards **yds.**, and grams **g.** I also learned about science **sci.**, adverbs **advs.**, and adjectives **adjs.** It was a boring trip!

We only traveled about two miles per hour **mph.** That's why it took us so long. Also, we stopped at a number **no.** of relatives' places and stayed for months **mos.** on end.

Next time let's fly!

Table of Contents.
1. On what page of the guide would you find what kind of fast-food places are in town? **20**
2. On what page would there be information about what the weather is like? **5**
3. You want to see if any good movies are playing; what page would you look under? **5**
4. You want to see if there are any job openings; what page would you look under? **17**
5. You want a copy of the bus schedule; what page would you find it on? **12**

Corvallis Happenings Guide
Local Information,
Table of Contents
Entertainment 5
Weather Conditions 5
Transportation 12
Careers and Employment 17
Dining Out 20

Page 51

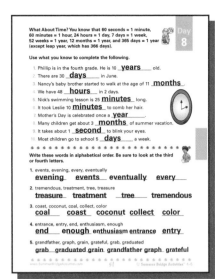

Day 8

What About Time? You know that 60 seconds = 1 minute, 60 minutes = 1 hour, 24 hours = 1 day, 7 days = 1 week, 52 weeks = 1 year, 12 months = 1 year, and 365 days = 1 year (except leap year, which has 366 days).

Use what you know to complete the following.
1. Phillip is in the fourth grade. He is 10 **years** old.
2. There are 30 **days** in June.
3. Nancy's baby brother started to walk at the age of 11 **months**.
4. We have 48 **hours** in 2 days.
5. Nick's swimming lesson is 25 **minutes** long.
6. It took Leslie 10 **minutes** to comb her hair.
7. Mother's Day is celebrated once a **year**.
8. Many children get about 3 **months** of summer vacation.
9. It takes about 1 **second** to blink your eyes.
10. Most children go to school 5 **days** a week.

Write these words in alphabetical order. Be sure to look at the third or fourth letters.
1. events, evening, every, eventually
evening events eventually every
2. tremendous, treatment, tree, treasure
treasure treatment tree tremendous
3. coast, coconut, coal, collect, color
coal coast coconut collect color
4. entrance, entry, end, enthusiasm, enough
end enough enthusiasm entrance entry
5. grandfather, graph, grain, grateful, grab, graduated
grab graduated grain grandfather graph grateful

Page 52

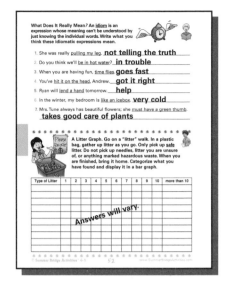

What Does It Really Mean? An **idiom** is an expression whose meaning can't be understood by just knowing the individual words. Write what you think these idiomatic expressions mean.

1. She was really pulling my leg. **not telling the truth**
2. Do you think we'll be in hot water? **in trouble**
3. When you are having fun, time flies. **goes fast**
4. You've hit it on the head, Andrew. **got it right**
5. Ryan will lend a hand tomorrow. **help**
6. In the winter, my bedroom is like an icebox. **very cold**
7. Mrs. Tune always has beautiful flowers; she must have a green thumb. **takes good care of plants**

A Litter Graph. Go on a "litter" walk. In a plastic bag, gather up litter as you go. Only pick up safe litter. Do not pick up needles, litter you are unsure of, or anything marked hazardous waste. When you are finished, bring it home. Categorize what you have found and display it in a bar graph.

Type of Litter	1	2	3	4	5	6	7	8	9	10	more than 10

Answers will vary.

Page 53

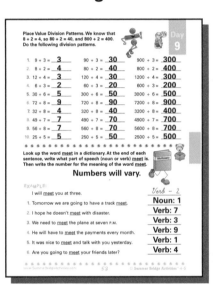

Day 9

Place Value Division Patterns. We know that 8 ÷ 2 = 4, so 80 ÷ 2 = 40, and 800 ÷ 2 = 400. Do the following division patterns.

1. 9 ÷ 3 = **3**, 90 ÷ 3 = **30**, 900 ÷ 3 = **300**
2. 8 ÷ 2 = **4**, 80 ÷ 2 = **40**, 800 ÷ 2 = **400**
3. 12 ÷ 4 = **3**, 120 ÷ 4 = **30**, 1200 ÷ 4 = **300**
4. 6 ÷ 3 = **2**, 60 ÷ 3 = **20**, 600 ÷ 3 = **200**
5. 30 ÷ 6 = **5**, 300 ÷ 6 = **50**, 3000 ÷ 6 = **500**
6. 72 ÷ 8 = **9**, 720 ÷ 8 = **90**, 7200 ÷ 8 = **900**
7. 32 ÷ 8 = **4**, 320 ÷ 8 = **40**, 3200 ÷ 8 = **400**
8. 49 ÷ 7 = **7**, 490 ÷ 7 = **70**, 4900 ÷ 7 = **700**
9. 56 ÷ 8 = **7**, 560 ÷ 8 = **70**, 5600 ÷ 8 = **700**
10. 25 ÷ 5 = **5**, 250 ÷ 5 = **50**, 2500 ÷ 5 = **500**

Look up the word **meet** in a dictionary. At the end of each sentence, write what part of speech (noun or verb) **meet** is. Then write the number for the meaning of the word **meet**.
Numbers will vary.

EXAMPLE: I will meet you at three. *Verb – 2*
1. Tomorrow we are going to have a track meet. **Noun: 1**
2. I hope he doesn't meet with disaster. **Verb: 7**
3. We need to meet the plane at seven P.M. **Verb: 3**
4. He will have to meet the payments every month. **Verb: 9**
5. It was nice to meet and talk with you yesterday. **Verb: 1**
6. Are you going to meet your friends later? **Verb: 4**

Page 54

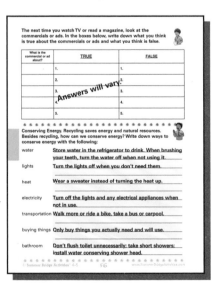

Someone or Something with Power. What is power? Choose something or someone with power. How do they have power? How did they get it? Could they lose it? How? Why? Do you have power? Yes you do! What are some of the powers that you have that you don't have that you would like to have?

SUPER STAR

Answers will vary.

Page 55

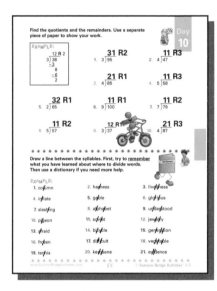

Day 10

Find the quotients and the remainders. Use a separate piece of paper to show your work.

EXAMPLE: 3)38 = 12 R2
1. 3)95 = **31 R2**
2. 4)47 = **11 R3**
3. 4)85 = **21 R1**
4. 5)58 = **11 R3**
5. 2)65 = **32 R1**
6. 9)100 = **11 R1**
7. 7)79 = **11 R2**
8. 5)57 = **11 R2**
9. 3)37 = **12 R1**
10. 4)87 = **21 R3**

Draw a line between the syllables. First, try to **remember** what you have learned about where to divide words. Then use a dictionary if you need more help.

EXAMPLE:
1. col|umn
2. har|ness
3. live|li|ness
4. in|flate
5. ga|ble
6. glo|ri|ous
7. slash|ing
8. al|pha|bet
9. un|der|stood
10. pi|geon
11. so|viet
12. jew|el|ry
13. a|fraid
14. bi|cy|cle
15. gen|er|a|tion
16. fro|zen
17. dif|fi|cult
18. veg|e|ta|ble
19. ten|nis
20. ker|o|sene
21. ev|i|dence

Page 56

The next time you watch TV or read a magazine, look at the commercials or ads. In the boxes below, write down what you think is true about the commercials or ads and what you think is false.

What is the commercial or ad about?	TRUE	FALSE
1.	1.	1.
2.	2.	2.
3.	3.	3.
4.	4.	4.

Answers will vary.

Conserving Energy. Recycling saves energy and natural resources. Besides recycling, how can we conserve energy? Write down ways to conserve energy with the following:

water — Store water in the refrigerator to drink. When brushing your teeth, turn the water off when not using it.
lights — Turn the lights off when you don't need them.
heat — Wear a sweater instead of turning the heat up.
electricity — Turn off the lights and any electrical appliances when not in use.
transportation — Walk more or ride a bike, take a bus or carpool.
buying things — Only buy things you actually need and will use.
bathroom — Don't flush toilet unnecessarily; take short showers; install water conserving shower head.

Page 57

Day 11

Write the fraction that describes the shaded section.

EXAMPLE:
1. 1/2
2. 1/4
3. 1/6
4.
5.
6.
7.
8.
9.
10.
11.
12.

Identify each angle and label it in the space below.

Right Angle—angle that measures 90 degrees (the angle forms a square corner)
Acute Angle—angle that measures less than a right angle, or less than 90 degrees
Obtuse Angle—angle that measures more than 90 degrees, or greater than a right angle

1. **Right Angle**
2. **Obtuse Angle**
3. **Acute Angle**
4. **Obtuse Angle**
5. **Acute Angle**
6. **Right Angle**

Page 58

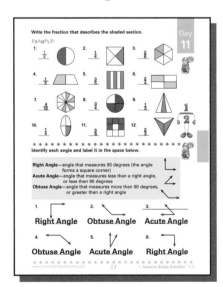

Practice writing and spelling these **homophones**. Write in cursive. After you know how to spell them, have someone give you a test to see if you can spell them without looking. Write each word twice.

way — tide
weigh — tied
base — waist
bass — waste
threw — sore
through — soar
scene — pare
seen — pair
sight — pear
site

Writing will vary.

Water in the Air. There is water in the air. How does it get there? Clouds and rain are made from water vapor in the air.

Try this to help explain how water gets into the air. Take 3 or more drinking glasses that are all about the same size. Fill the glasses almost full of water. Place them in different areas, such as warm places, cool places, dark places, windy places, outside places, inside places, and other places of your choice. Watch them for 4 or 5 days or longer. Check the water levels. What happened to the water in the glasses? Where did it go? Explain in your own words where you think the water vapor in the atmosphere comes from and where it goes.

Answers will vary.

Page 59

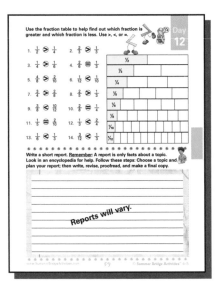

Day 12

Use the fraction table to help find out which fraction is greater and which fraction is less. Use >, <, or =.

1. $\frac{1}{2}$ > $\frac{1}{4}$ 2. $\frac{2}{3}$ > $\frac{1}{3}$
3. $\frac{1}{4}$ < $\frac{1}{2}$ 4. $\frac{6}{8}$ = $\frac{3}{4}$
5. $\frac{4}{8}$ < $\frac{6}{10}$ 6. $\frac{1}{12}$ < $\frac{4}{10}$
7. $\frac{3}{4}$ > $\frac{2}{8}$ 8. $\frac{5}{8}$ > $\frac{1}{3}$
9. $\frac{3}{8}$ < $\frac{9}{10}$ 10. $\frac{2}{8}$ < $\frac{1}{3}$
11. $\frac{1}{8}$ < $\frac{6}{10}$ 12. $\frac{1}{3}$ < $\frac{3}{4}$
13. $\frac{1}{8}$ < $\frac{1}{3}$ 14. $\frac{3}{12}$ < $\frac{1}{3}$

Write a short report. Remember: A report is only facts about a topic. Look in an encyclopedia for help. Follow these steps: Choose a topic and plan your report; then write, revise, proofread, and make a final copy.

Reports will vary.

Page 60

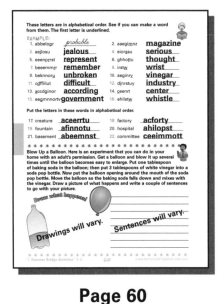

These letters are in alphabetical order. See if you can make a word from them. The first letter is underlined.

EXAMPLE: abbelogr — *probable*

1. abbelogr — *probable*
2. aaegimnz — **magazine**
3. aejlosu — **jealous**
4. eiorgsu — **serious**
5. eeenprst — **represent**
6. ghhottu — **thought**
7. beeemmrr — **remember**
8. irstw — **wrist**
9. beknnoru — **unbroken**
10. aeginry — **vinegar**
11. cgffilut — **difficult**
12. djnrstuy — **industry**
13. accdginor — **according**
14. ceenrt — **center**
15. eegmnnortv — **government**
16. ehilstw — **whistle**

Put the letters in these words in alphabetical order.

17. creature — **aceerrtu**
18. factory — **acforty**
19. fountain — **afinnotu**
20. hospital — **ahilopst**
21. basement — **abeemnst**
22. committee — **ceeiimott**

Blow Up a Balloon. Here is an experiment that you can do in your home with an adult's permission. Get a balloon and blow it up several times until the balloon becomes easy to enlarge. Put one tablespoon of baking soda in the balloon; then put 3 tablespoons of white vinegar into a soda pop bottle. Now put the balloon opening around the mouth of the soda pop bottle. Move the balloon so the baking soda falls down and mixes with the vinegar. Draw a picture of what happens and write a couple of sentences to go with your picture.

Draw what happens!
Drawings will vary.
Sentences will vary.

Page 61

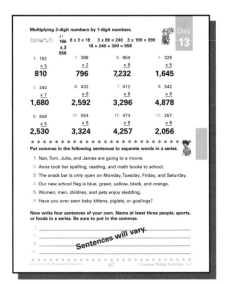

Day 13

Multiplying 3-digit numbers by 1-digit numbers.

EXAMPLE: $186 \times 3 = 558$ $6 \times 3 = 18$ $3 \times 80 = 240$ $3 \times 100 = 300$ $18 + 240 + 300 = 558$

1. 162 × 5	2. 398 × 2	3. 904 × 8	4. 329 × 5
810	796	7,232	1,645

5. 240 × 7	6. 432 × 6	7. 412 × 8	8. 542 × 9
1,680	2,592	3,296	4,878

9. 506 × 5	10. 554 × 6	11. 473 × 9	12. 257 × 8
2,530	3,324	4,257	2,056

Put commas in the following sentences to separate words in a series.

1. Nan, Tom, Julie, and James are going to a movie.
2. Anne took her spelling, reading, and math books to school.
3. The snack bar is only open on Monday, Tuesday, Friday, and Saturday.
4. Our new school flag is blue, green, yellow, black, and orange.
5. Women, men, children, and pets enjoy sledding.
6. Have you ever seen baby kittens, piglets, or goslings?

Now write four sentences of your own. Name at least three people, sports, or foods in a series. Be sure to put in the commas.

Sentences will vary.

Page 62

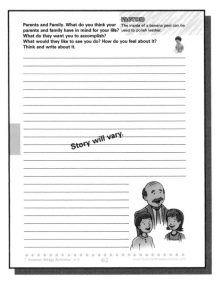

Parents and Family. What do you think your parents and family have in mind for your life? What do they want you to accomplish? What would they like to see you do? How do you feel about it? Think and write about it.

FACTOID The inside of a banana peel can be used to polish leather.

Story will vary.

Page 63

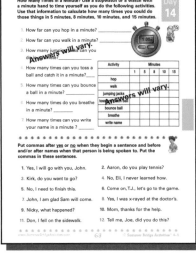

Day 14

How Many Times in a Minute? Use a stopwatch or a watch with a minute hand to time yourself as you do the following activities. Use that information to calculate how many times you could do those things in 5 minutes, 8 minutes, 10 minutes, and 15 minutes.

1. How far can you hop in a minute?
2. How far can you walk in a minute?
3. How many jumping jacks can you do in a minute?
4. How many times can you toss a ball and catch it in a minute?
5. How many times can you bounce a ball in a minute?
6. How many times do you breathe in a minute?
7. How many times can you write your name in a minute?

Answers will vary.

Activity	Minutes				
	1	5	8	10	15
hop					
walk					
jumping jacks					
toss ball					
bounce ball					
breathe					
write name					

Put commas after yes or no when they begin a sentence and before and/or after names when that person is being spoken to. Put the commas in these sentences.

1. Yes, I will go with you, John.
2. Aaron, do you play tennis?
3. Kirk, do you want to go?
4. No, Eli, I never learned how.
5. No, I need to finish this.
6. Come on, T.J., let's go to the game.
7. John, I am glad Sam will come.
8. Yes, I was x-rayed at the doctor's.
9. Nicky, what happened?
10. Mom, thanks for the help.
11. Don, I fell on the sidewalk.
12. Tell me, Joe, did you do this?

Page 64

Do you know when the holidays come? Fill in the blanks with the date or name of the correct holiday. Use a calendar if you need help.

1. Many children look forward to **Hanukkah** or **Christmas** in December.
2. On January 1 we celebrate **New Year's Day**.
3. In May we have **Mother's Day**.
4. Be sure to wear green in March. It's **St. Patrick's Day**.
5. In October 1492 he sailed the ocean blue. **Columbus Day**
6. On February 14 be sure to send your sweetheart a **Valentine**.
7. On July 4 we celebrate **Independence Day**.
8. October 31 can be really scary. **Halloween**
9. Sometimes it comes in March; sometimes it comes in April: **Easter**
10. Do you work on **Labor Day** in September?
11. **Washington** and **Lincoln** also have birthdays in February.
12. In June we also have **Father's Day**.
13. Martin Luther King Jr.'s birthday is in **January**.
14. Because the Pilgrims came, we have **Thanksgiving**.
15. **Flag Day** is in June.
16. On November 11 we honor our **Veterans**.

At the top of each page in a dictionary you will find two guide words. The guide word on the left tells you the first word found on the page. The guide word on the right tells you the last word found on the page. Circle the word that will be found on the page with the following guide words.

1. bowling–brain: bread (braid) brawl
2. monster–mope: morbid monsoon (moor)
3. golem–gossamer: (gondola) goal gourd
4. flank–flaw: (flash) flame flight
5. liquid–litter: (lists) live lion
6. work–worst: word (world) worth
7. spoon–spread: spoil sprite (spray)
8. central–chafe: cell chalet (certain)

Page 65

Day 15

Draw a new figure by following the directions given.

1. Flip horizontally.
2. Turn 180° ($\frac{1}{2}$ turn).
3. Flip vertically.
4. Turn 90° ($\frac{1}{4}$ turn).
5. Flip vertically, turn 90°.
6. Turn 270° ($\frac{3}{4}$ turn).

Using Punctuation Marks. Put periods and question, exclamation, and quotation marks in the following sentences. Use proper capitalization.

1. "Nate, do you have the map of our town?" asked Kit.
2. "What an exciting day I had!" cried Mary.
3. I said, "The puppy fell into the well!"
4. "Did you learn that birds' bones are hollow?" asked Mrs. Tippy.
5. She answered, "No, I did not learn that."
6. Wayne exclaimed, "I won first prize for the pie eating contest!"
7. "I'm tired of all work and no play," said Sadie.
8. "I agree with you," replied Sarah.
9. Mr. Harris said, "This assignment is due tomorrow."
10. "It will be part of your final grade," he added.

Page 66

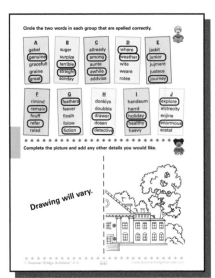

Circle the two words in each group that are spelled correctly.

A. gabel (genuine) (gracefull) graine (great)
B. (suger) surpize (terrible) (aunte) sonday
C. (already) among wite (awhile) addvise
D. (where) (weather) weare rotee
E. (jackit) (junior) juujment justece (journey)
F. rimind (remain) fouff (refer) raisd
G. (feathers) feever finsih folow (fiction)
H. donkiys doubble (drawer) dosen (detective)
I. handsum herrd (holiday) (healthy) haevy
J. (explore) elctrecity enjine (enormous) ecstat

Complete the picture and add any other details you would like.

Drawing will vary.

Page 67

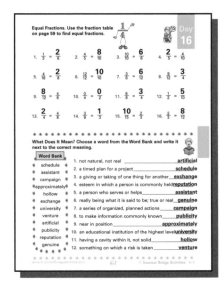

Day 16

Equal Fractions. Use the fraction table on page 59 to find equal fractions.

1. $\frac{1}{3} = \frac{2}{6}$
2. $\frac{4}{5} = \frac{8}{10}$
3. $\frac{3}{10} = \frac{6}{?}$
4. $\frac{2}{5} = \frac{4}{10}$
5. $\frac{4}{16} = \frac{2}{?}$
6. $\frac{5}{6} = \frac{10}{?}$
7. $\frac{3}{6} = \frac{6}{12}$
8. $\frac{1}{4} = \frac{3}{12}$
9. $\frac{8}{12} = \frac{2}{?}$
10. $\frac{1}{6} = \frac{0}{?}$
11. $\frac{1}{4} = \frac{3}{12}$
12. $\frac{1}{2} = \frac{5}{10}$
13. $\frac{2}{4} = \frac{1}{2}$
14. $\frac{3}{5} = \frac{?}{15}$
15. $\frac{10}{15} = \frac{2}{?}$
16. $\frac{2}{3} = \frac{8}{12}$

What Does It Mean? Choose a word from the Word Bank and write it next to the correct meaning.

Word Bank
schedule, assistant, campaign, approximately, hollow, exchange, university, venture, artificial, publicity, reputation, genuine

1. not natural, not real — **artificial**
2. a timed plan for a project — **schedule**
3. a giving or taking of one thing for another — **exchange**
4. esteem in which a person is commonly held — **reputation**
5. a person who serves or helps — **assistant**
6. really being what it is said to be; true or real — **genuine**
7. a series of organized, planned actions — **campaign**
8. to make information commonly known — **publicity**
9. near in position — **approximately**
10. an educational institution of the highest level — **university**
11. having a cavity within it, not solid — **hollow**
12. something on which a risk is taken — **venture**

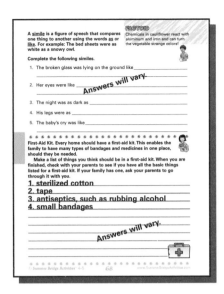

Page 68

A *simile* is a figure of speech that compares one thing to another using the words as or like. For example: The bed sheets were as white as a snowy owl.

FACTOID
Chemicals in cauliflower react with aluminum and iron and can turn the vegetable strange colors!

Complete the following similes.

1. The broken glass was lying on the ground like _____
2. Her eyes were like _____ Answers will vary.
3. The night was as dark as _____
4. His legs were as _____
5. The baby's cry was like _____

First-Aid Kit. Every home should have a first-aid kit. This enables the family to have many types of bandages and medicines in one place, should they be needed.
Make a list of things you think should be in a first-aid kit. When you are finished, check with your parents to see if you have all the basic things listed for a first-aid kit. If your family has one, ask your parents to go through it with you.

1. sterilized cotton
2. tape
3. antiseptics, such as rubbing alcohol
4. small bandages
_____
_____
Answers will vary.

Page 69

Adding Fractions.

$\frac{1}{3} + \frac{2}{3} = \frac{3}{3}$ ← add the numerator, use the same denominator

1. $\frac{1}{3} + \frac{1}{3} = \frac{2}{3}$ 2. $\frac{1}{2} + \frac{1}{2} = \frac{2}{2}$ 3. $\frac{6}{12} + \frac{5}{12} = \frac{11}{12}$ 4. $\frac{11}{12} + \frac{11}{12} = \frac{22}{11}$

5. $\frac{6}{8} + \frac{2}{8} = \frac{8}{8}$ 6. $\frac{3}{10} + \frac{4}{10} = \frac{7}{10}$ 7. $\frac{1}{6} + \frac{2}{6} = \frac{3}{6}$ 8. $\frac{5}{10} + \frac{3}{10} = \frac{8}{10}$

9. $\frac{1}{4} + \frac{2}{4} = \frac{3}{4}$ 10. $\frac{1}{8} + \frac{5}{8} = \frac{6}{8}$ 11. $\frac{3}{5} + \frac{1}{5} = \frac{4}{5}$ 12. $\frac{2}{8} + \frac{4}{8} = \frac{6}{8}$

13. $\frac{3}{6} + \frac{1}{6} = \frac{4}{6}$ 14. $\frac{4}{12} + \frac{5}{12} = \frac{9}{12}$ 15. $\frac{3}{8} + \frac{5}{8} = \frac{8}{8}$ 16. $\frac{6}{12} + \frac{5}{12} = \frac{11}{12}$

Circle the abbreviations in these sentences.
Remember: Abbreviations are short forms of words and usually begin with capital letters and end with periods.

1. Dr. Cox is my family doctor.
2. Do you live on Rocksberry Rd.?
3. My teacher's name is Ms. Hansen.
4. On Mon. we are taking a trip to Fort Worth Tx.
5. Will Mr. Harris sell his company to your parents?

Now write the abbreviations for these words.

6. avenue — Ave.
7. Tuesday — Tues.
8. postscript — p.s.
9. Mister — Mr.
10. teaspoon — tsp.
11. tablespoon — Tbs.
12. January — Jan.
13. circle — Cir.
14. Thursday — Thur.
15. company — Co.

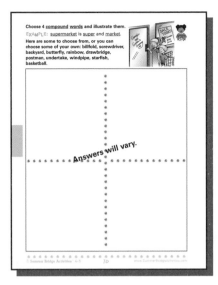

Page 70

Choose 4 compound words and illustrate them.
EXAMPLE: supermarket is super and market.
Here are some to choose from, or you can choose some of your own: billfold, screwdriver, backyard, butterfly, rainbow, drawbridge, postman, undertake, windpipe, starfish, basketball.

Answers will vary.

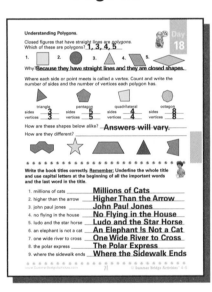

Page 71

Understanding Polygons.
Closed figures that have straight lines are polygons.
Which of these are polygons? 1, 3, 4, 5

Why? Because they have straight lines and they are closed shapes.

Where each side or point meets is called a vertex. Count and write the number of sides and the number of vertices each shape has.

triangle — sides 3, vertices 3
pentagon — sides 5, vertices 5
quadrilateral — sides 4, vertices 4
octagon — sides 8, vertices 8

How are these shapes below alike? Answers will vary.
How are they different?

Write the book titles correctly. Remember: Underline the whole title and use capital letters at the beginning of all the important words and the last word in the title.

1. millions of cats — Millions of Cats
2. higher than the arrow — Higher Than the Arrow
3. john paul jones — John Paul Jones
4. no flying in the house — No Flying in the House
5. ludo and the star horse — Ludo and the Star Horse
6. an elephant is not a cat — An Elephant Is Not a Cat
7. one wide river to cross — One Wide River to Cross
8. the polar express — The Polar Express
9. where the sidewalk ends — Where the Sidewalk Ends

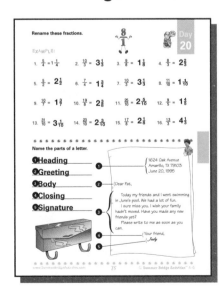

Page 72

Neighborhood Survey. Conduct a survey with your neighborhood, friends, or relatives. Find out how many have pets. If possible, observe them with their pets. Do they keep their pets inside or outside? Are their food provided for them? How much space do they have to move around in? Think of other questions you might ask. Record your information in a report, chart, graph, table, or picture.

Answers will vary.

Page 73

Use what you know about polygons to make a pattern. Start with one polygon and flip, turn, or slide it to make a pattern.
EXAMPLE:

or

Now try your hand at making some polygon patterns.

Drawings will vary.

Review of Homonyms or Homophones. Write 5 sentences using some of these pairs of homonyms or homophones. Be sure to use both words and underline them.
EXAMPLE: Would you chop some wood?

1. no, know   2. four, for   3. way, weigh
4. ate, eight   5. sun, son   6. sent, cent
7. see, sea   8. tail, tale   9. rode, road
10. knight, night   11. sale, sail   12. pair, pear
13. new, knew   14. so, sew   15. their, there

Here are some examples:
1. My sailboat is for sale.
2. I knew I needed to practice the new words.
3. Their house is over there.
4. Where is the shirt I'm going to wear?
5. No, I don't know how to ride a bike!

Answers will vary.

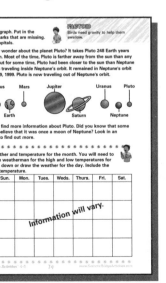

Page 74

Read this paragraph. Put in the punctuation marks that are missing. Don't forget capitals.

FACTOID
Birds need gravity to help them swallow.

Do you ever wonder about the planet Pluto? It takes Pluto 248 Earth years to orbit the sun. Most of the time, Pluto is farther away from the sun than any other planet. But for some time, Pluto had been closer to the sun than Neptune because it was traveling inside Neptune's orbit. It remained in Neptune's orbit until February 9, 1999. Pluto is now traveling out of Neptune's orbit.

Sun — Mercury, Venus, Earth, Mars, Jupiter, Saturn, Uranus, Neptune, Pluto

See if you can find more information about Pluto. Did you know that some astronomers believe that it was once a moon of Neptune? Look in an encyclopedia to find out more.

Chart the weather and temperature for the month. You will need to check with the weatherman for the high and low temperatures for the day. Write down or draw the weather for the day. Include the high and low temperature.

	Sun.	Mon.	Tues.	Weds.	Thurs.	Fri.	Sat.

Information will vary.

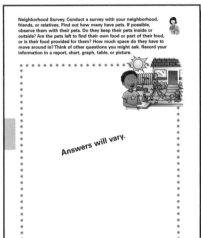

Page 75

Rename these fractions.

$\frac{8}{1}$

EXAMPLE: $\frac{5}{4} = 1\frac{1}{4}$

1. $\frac{5}{4} = 1\frac{1}{4}$ 2. $\frac{10}{3} = 3\frac{1}{3}$ 3. $\frac{9}{8} = 1\frac{1}{8}$ 4. $\frac{8}{3} = 2\frac{2}{3}$

5. $\frac{5}{2} = 2\frac{1}{2}$ 6. $\frac{7}{4} = 1\frac{3}{4}$ 7. $\frac{10}{3} = 3\frac{1}{3}$ 8. $\frac{11}{10} = 1\frac{1}{10}$

9. $\frac{10}{7} = 1\frac{3}{7}$ 10. $\frac{18}{8} = 2\frac{2}{8}$ 11. $\frac{28}{10} = 2\frac{8}{10}$ 12. $\frac{9}{5} = 1\frac{4}{5}$

13. $\frac{31}{10} = 3\frac{1}{10}$ 14. $\frac{23}{8} = 2\frac{7}{8}$ 15. $\frac{17}{7} = 2\frac{3}{7}$ 16. $\frac{13}{3} = 4\frac{1}{3}$

Name the parts of a letter.

❶ Heading
❷ Greeting
❸ Body
❹ Closing
❺ Signature

1624 Oak Avenue
Amarillo, TX 79103
June 20, 1995

Dear Pat,

Today my friend and I went swimming in June's pool. We had a lot of fun.
I sure miss you. I wish your family hadn't moved. Have you made any new friends yet?
Please write to me as soon as you can.

Your friend,
Judy

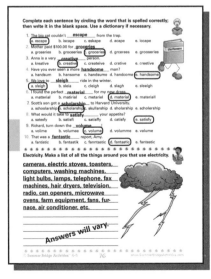

Page 76

Complete each sentence by circling the word that is spelled correctly; then write it in the blank space. Use a dictionary if necessary.

1. The big cat couldn't escape from the trap.
   a. escape   b. iscape   c. eskape   d. acape   e. iccape
2. Mother paid $100.00 for groceries.
   a. groceries   b. grocerries   c. groceries   d. grcerees   e. grooseries
3. Anna is a very creative person.
   a. kreative   b. creative   c. createve   d. crative   e. creativ
4. Have you ever seen a more handsome man?
   a. handsum   b. hansome   c. handsome   d. handcome   e. handsome
5. We love to sleigh ride in the winter.
   a. sleigh   b. sleia   c. cleigh   d. slagh   e. sleiigh
6. I found the perfect material for my new dress.
   a. material   b. materal   c. meterial   d. material   e. materiall
7. Scott's son got a scholarship to Harvard University.
   a. scholarship   b. scholarship   c. skullarship   d. shcolarship   e. scholorship
8. What would it take to satisfy your appetite?
   a. satesfy   b. satisfi   c. satisfy   d. catisfy   e. satisfy
9. Richard, turn down the volume.
   a. volime   b. volumee   c. volume   d. volumme   e. volume
10. That was a fantastic report, Amy.
    a. fantastic   b. fantastik   c. fanntastic   d. fantastic   e. fantestic

Electricity. Make a list of all the things around you that use electricity.

cameras, electric stoves, toasters, computers, washing machines, light bulbs, lamps, telephone, fax machines, hair dryers, television, radio, can openers, microwave ovens, farm equipment, furnace, air conditioner, etc.

Answers will vary.

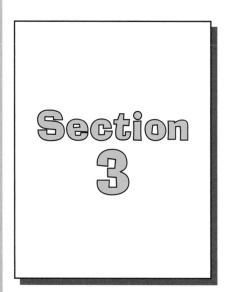

Section 3

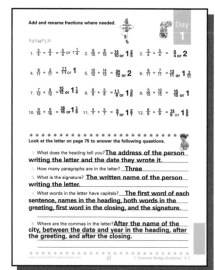

Page 81

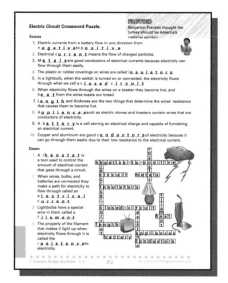

Page 82

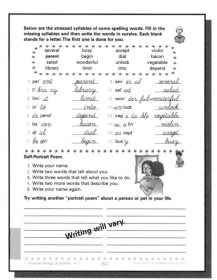

Page 83

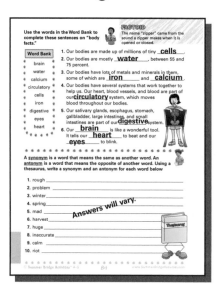

Page 84

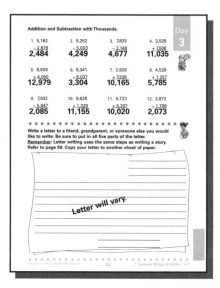

Page 85

Page 86

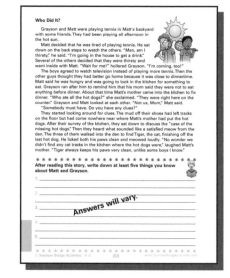

Page 87

Who Did It?

Page 88

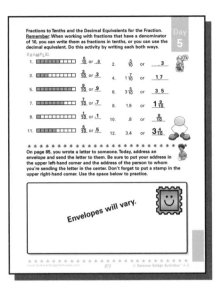

Page 89

Fractions to Tenths and the Decimal Equivalents for the Fraction.
Remember: When working with fractions that have a denominator of 10, you can write them as fractions in tenths, or you can use the decimal equivalent. Do this activity by writing each both ways.

EXAMPLE:
1. ▭ 6/10 or .6
2. 3/10 or .3
3. 7/10 or 1.7
4. 1 1/10
5. ▭ 9/10 or .9
6. 3 5/10 or 3 5/10
7. ▭ 7/10 or .7
8. 1.9 or 1 9/10
9. ▭ 1/10 or .1
10. .8 or 8/10
11. ▭ 5/10 or .5
12. 3.4 or 3 4/10

On page 85, you wrote a letter to someone. Today, address an envelope and send the letter to them. Be sure to put your address in the upper left-hand corner and the address of the person to whom you're sending the letter in the center. Don't forget to put a stamp in the upper right-hand corner. Use the space below to practice.

Envelopes will vary.

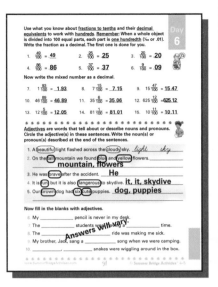

Page 91

Use what you know about fractions to tenths and their decimal equivalents to work with hundreds. Remember: When a whole object is divided into 100 equal parts, each part is one hundredth (1/100 or .01). Write the fraction as a decimal. The first one is done for you.

1. 49/100 = .49
2. 25/100 = .25
3. 20/100 = .20
4. 86/100 = .86
5. 37/100 = .37
6. 9/100 = .09

Now write the mixed number as a decimal.

7. 1 93/100 = 1.93
8. 7 15/100 = 7.15
9. 15 47/100 = 15.47
10. 46 89/100 = 46.89
11. 35 6/100 = 35.06
12. 625 12/100 = 625.12
13. 12 5/100 = 12.05
14. 81 1/100 = 81.01
15. 10 11/100 = 10.11

Adjectives are words that tell about or describe nouns and pronouns. Circle the adjective(s) in these sentences. Write the noun(s) or pronoun(s) described at the end of the sentences.

1. A beautiful light flashed across the cloudy sky. **light, sky**
2. On the tall mountain we found blue and yellow flowers. **mountain, flowers**
3. He was brave after the accident. **He**
4. It is fun but it is also dangerous to skydive. **it, it, skydive**
5. Our brown dog had six cute puppies. **dog, puppies**

Now fill in the blanks with adjectives.

6. My _____ pencil is never in my desk.
7. The _____ students _____ time.
8. The _____ ride was making me sick.
9. My brother, Jack, sang a _____ song when we were camping.
10. _____ snakes were wiggling around in the box.

Answers will vary.

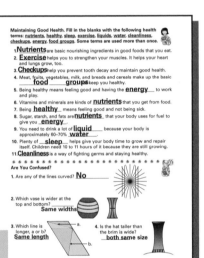

Page 92

Maintaining Good Health. Fill in the blanks with the following health terms: nutrients, healthy, sleep, exercise, liquids, water, cleanliness, checkups, energy, food groups. Some terms are used more than once.

1. **Nutrients** are basic nourishing ingredients in good foods that you eat.
2. **Exercise** helps you to strengthen your muscles. It helps your heart and lungs grow, too.
3. **Checkups** help you prevent tooth decay and maintain good health.
4. Meat, fruits, vegetables, milk, and breads and cereals make up the basic **food groups** keep you healthy.
5. Being healthy means feeling good and having the **energy** to work and play.
6. Vitamins and minerals are kinds of **nutrients** that you get from food.
7. Being **healthy** means feeling good and not being sick.
8. Sugar, starch, and fats are **nutrients** that your body uses for fuel to give you **energy**.
9. You need to drink a lot of **liquid** because your body is approximately 60–70% **water**.
10. Plenty of **sleep** helps give your body time to grow and repair itself. Children need 10 to 11 hours of it because they are still growing.
11. **Cleanliness** is a way of fighting germs and staying healthy.

Are You Confused?

1. Are any of the lines curved? **No**

2. Which vase is wider at the top and bottom? **Same widths**

3. Which line is longer, a or b? **Same length**

4. Is the hat taller than the brim is wide? **both same size**

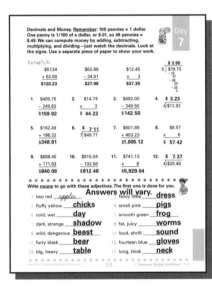

Page 93

Decimals and Money. Remember: 100 pennies = 1 dollar. One penny is 1/100 of a dollar, or $.01, so 49 pennies = $.49. We can compute money by adding, subtracting, multiplying, and dividing—just watch the decimals. Look at the signs. Use a separate piece of paper to show your work.

EXAMPLE:
$57.34 + $62.89 = $120.23
$62.89 − $34.91 = $27.98
$12.45 × $37.35 = $37.35
$19.75 ÷ 5 = $3.95

1. $409.75 − $249.83 = $159.92
2. $14.74 × 3 = $44.22
3. $492.00 − $349.50 = $142.50
4. $12.92 ÷ 4 = $3.23

5. $162.49 + $186.32 = $348.81
6. $49.77 ÷ 7 = $7.11
7. $601.89 + $403.23 = $1,005.12
8. $9.57 × 6 = $57.42

9. $668.45 + $171.63 = $840.08
10. $915.04 − $102.56 = $812.48
11. $741.13 × 8 = $5,929.04
12. $29.48 ÷ 4 = $7.37

Write nouns to go with these adjectives. The first one is done for you.

1. two red **apples**
2. fancy little **dress**
3. fluffy yellow **chicks**
4. small pink **pigs**
5. cold, wet **day**
6. smooth green **frog**
7. dark, strange **shadow**
8. fat, juicy **worms**
9. wild, dangerous **beast**
10. loud, shrill **sound**
11. furry black **bear**
12. fourteen blue **gloves**
13. big, heavy **table**
14. long, thick **neck**

Answers will vary.

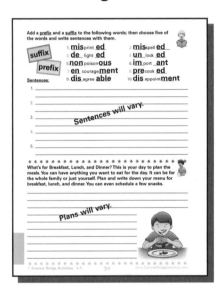

Page 94

Add a prefix and a suffix to the following words; then choose five of the words and write sentences with them.

suffix
prefix

1. mis print ed
2. mis spell ed
3. de light ed
4. un lock ed
5. non poison ous
6. im port ant
7. en courage ment
8. pre cook ed
9. dis agree able
10. dis appoint ment

Sentences:
1.
2.
3.
4.
5.

Sentences will vary.

What's for Breakfast, Lunch, and Dinner? This is your day to plan the meals. You can have anything you want to eat for the day. It can be for the whole family or just yourself. Plan and write down your menu for breakfast, lunch, and dinner. You can even schedule a few snacks.

Plans will vary.

Page 95

Multiplying Multiples of 10 and 100.
To use shortcuts to find the product of multiples of 10 or 100, write the product for the basic fact and count the zeros in the factors.
10 × 8 = 80 (1 zero) 10 × 80 = 800 (2 zeros) 10 × 800 = 8,000 (3 zeros)

Multiples of tens:
1. 10 × 5 = **50**
2. 7 × 10 = **70**
3. 39 × 10 = **390**
4. 30 × 30 = **900**
5. 54 × 10 = **540**
6. 10 × 21 = **210**
7. 710 × 10 = **7,100**
8. 9 × 10 = **90**
9. 70 × 30 = **2,100**

Multiples of hundreds:
10. 900 × 40 = **36,000**
11. 600 × 10 = **6,000**
12. 230 × 20 = **4,600**
13. 700 × 80 = **56,000**
14. 500 × 50 = **25,000**
15. 600 × 90 = **54,000**
16. 440 × 30 = **13,200**
17. 700 × 60 = **42,000**

Adjectives are used to compare. Add -er and -est to these adjectives.

EXAMPLE: red   redder   reddest
1. hot   **hotter**   **hottest**
2. nice   **nicer**   **nicest**
3. warm   **warmer**   **warmest**
4. hard   **harder**   **hardest**
5. easy   **easier**   **easiest**

Now write a story. Use as many of the adjectives above as you can. Underline the adjectives.

Story will vary.

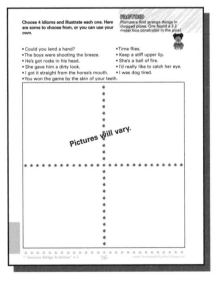

Page 96

Choose 4 idioms and illustrate each one. Here are some to choose from, or you can use your own.

FACTOID Plumbers find strange things in clogged pipes. One found a 2.2 meter boa constrictor in the pipe!

- Could you lend a hand?
- The boys were shooting the breeze.
- He's got rocks in his head.
- She gave him a dirty look.
- I got it straight from the horse's mouth.
- You won the game by the skin of your teeth.
- Time flies.
- Keep a stiff upper lip.
- She's a ball of fire.
- It'd really like to catch her eye.
- I was dog tired.

Pictures will vary.

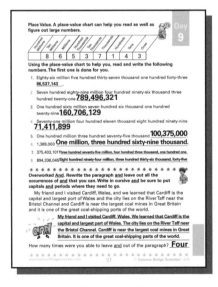

Page 97

Place Value. A place-value chart can help you read as well as figure out large numbers.

Hundred Millions	Ten Millions	Millions	Hundred Thousands	Ten Thousands	Thousands	Hundreds	Tens	Ones
8	6	5	3	7	1	4	3	

Using the place-value chart to help you, read and write the following numbers. The first one is done for you.

1. Eighty-six million five hundred thirty-seven thousand one hundred forty-three **86,537,143**
2. Seven hundred eighty-nine million four hundred ninety-six thousand three hundred twenty-one **789,496,321**
3. One hundred sixty million seven hundred six thousand one hundred twenty-nine **160,706,129**
4. Seventy-one million four hundred eleven thousand eight hundred ninety-nine **71,411,899**
5. One hundred million three hundred seventy-five thousand **100,375,000**
6. 1,369,000 **One million, three hundred sixty-nine thousand.**
7. 375,403,101 **Three hundred seventy-five million, four hundred three thousand, one hundred one.**
8. 894,336,045 **Eight hundred ninety-four million, three hundred thirty-six thousand, forty-five**

Overworked And. Rewrite the paragraph and leave out all the occurrences of and that you can. Write in cursive and be sure to put capitals and periods where they need to go.

My friend and I visited Cardiff, Wales, and we learned that Cardiff is the capital and largest port of Wales and the city lies on the River Taff near the Bristol Channel and Cardiff is near the largest coal mines in Great Britain and it is one of the great coal-shipping ports of the world.

My friend and I visited Cardiff, Wales. We learned that Cardiff is the capital and largest part of Wales. The city lies on the River Taff near the Bristol Channel. Cardiff is near the largest coal mines in Great Britain. It is one of the great coal-shipping ports of the world.

How many times were you able to leave and out of the paragraph? **Four**

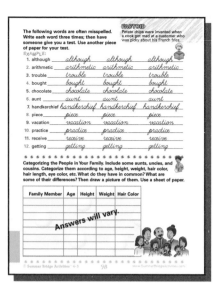

Page 98

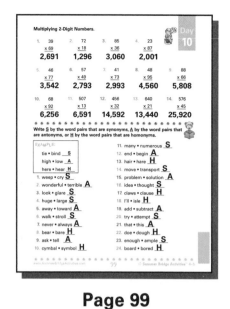

Page 99

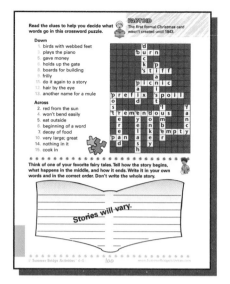

Page 100

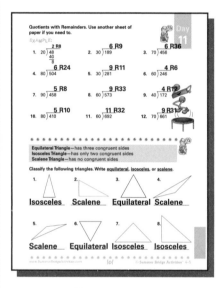

Page 101

Page 102

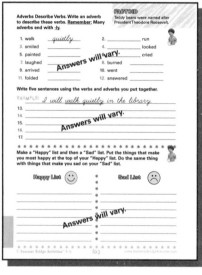

Page 103

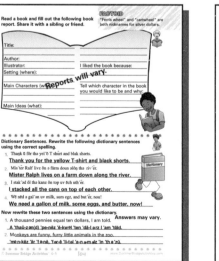

Page 104

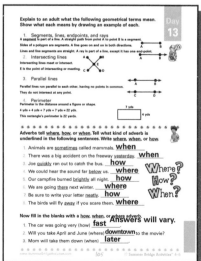

Page 105

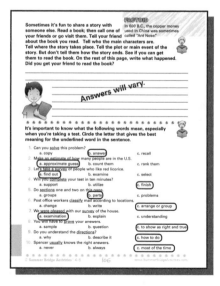

Page 106

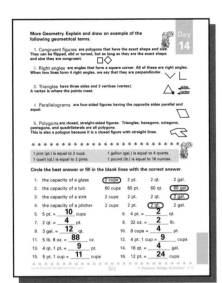

Page 107

More Geometry. Explain and draw an example of the following geometrical terms.

1. Congruent figures are polygons that have the exact shape and size. They can be flipped, slid or turned, but as long as they are the exact shape and size they are congruent.

2. Right angles are angles that form a square corner. All of these are right angles. When two lines form 4 right angles, we say that they are perpendicular.

3. Triangles have three sides and 3 vertices (vertex). A vertex is where the points meet.

4. Parallelograms are four-sided figures having the opposite sides parallel and equal.

5. Polygons are closed, straight-sided figures. Triangles, hexagons, octagons, pentagons, and quadrilaterals are all polygons. This is also a polygon because it is a closed figure with straight lines.

1 pint (pt.) is equal to 2 cups. 1 gallon (gal.) is equal to 4 quarts.
1 quart (qt.) is equal to 2 pints. 1 pound (lb.) is equal to 16 ounces.

Circle the best answer or fill in the blank lines with the correct answer.

1. the capacity of a glass — **2 cups** · 2 pt. · 2 qt. · 2 gal.
2. the capacity of a tub — 60 cups · 60 pt. · 60 qt. · **60 gal.**
3. the capacity of a sink — 2 cups · 2 pt. · 2 qt. · **2 gal.**
4. the capacity of a pitcher — 2 cups · 2 pt. · **2 qt.** · 2 gal.
5. 5 pt. = **10** cups
6. 4 pt. = **2** qt.
7. 2 qt. = **4** pt.
8. 32 oz. = **2** lb.
9. 3 gal. = **12** qt.
10. 8 cups = **4** pt.
11. 5 lb. 8 oz. = **88** oz.
12. 4 pt. 1 cup = **9** cups
13. 4 qt. 1 pt. = **9** pt.
14. 16 qt. = **4** gal.
15. 5 pt. 1 cup = **11** cups
16. 12 pt. = **24** cups

107

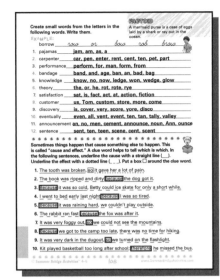

Page 108

Create small words from the letters in the following words. Write them.

FACTOID — A mermaid purse is a case of eggs laid by a shark or ray out in the ocean.

EXAMPLE:
borrow — row, or, bow, rob, brow

1. pajamas — jam, am, as, a
2. carpenter — car, pen, enter, rent, cent, ten, pet, part
3. performance — perform, for, man, form, from
4. bandage — band, and, age, ban, an, bad, bag
5. knowledge — know, no, now, ledge, won, wedge, glow
6. theory — the, or, he, rot, rote, rye
7. satisfaction — sat, is, fact, act, at, action, fiction
8. customer — us, Tom, custom, store, more, come
9. discovery — is, cover, very, score, yore, disco
10. eventually — even, all, vent, event, ten, tan, tally, valley
11. announcement — an, no, men, cement, announce, noun, Ann, ounce
12. sentence — sent, ten, teen, scene, cent, scent

Sometimes things happen that cause something else to happen. This is called "cause and effect." A clue word helps to tell which is which. In the following sentences, underline the cause with a straight line (___). Underline the effect with a dotted line (___). Put a box ☐ around the clue word.

1. The tooth was broken, so it gave her a lot of pain.
2. The book was ripped and dirty because the dog got it.
3. Because it was so cold, Betty could ice skate for only a short while.
4. I went to bed early last night because I was so tired.
5. Because it was raining hard, we couldn't play outside.
6. The rabbit ran fast because the fox was after it.
7. It was very foggy out, so we could not see the mountains.
8. Because we got to the camp too late, there was no time for hiking.
9. It was very dark in the dugout, so we turned on the flashlight.
10. Kit played basketball too long after school; therefore he missed the bus.

108

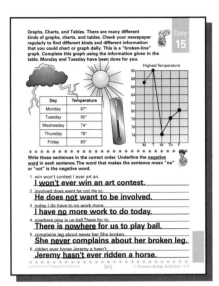

Page 109

Graphs, Charts, and Tables. There are many different kinds of graphs, charts, and tables. Check your newspaper regularly to find different kinds and different information that you could chart or graph daily. This is a "broken-line" graph. Complete this graph using the information given in the table. Monday and Tuesday have been done for you.

Day	Temperature
Monday	87°
Tuesday	90°
Wednesday	74°
Thursday	78°
Friday	80°

Write these sentences in the correct order. Underline the negative word in each sentence. The word that makes the sentence mean "no" or "not" is the negative word.

1. win won't contest I ever art an.
I won't ever win an art contest.
2. involved does want be not He to.
He does not want to be involved.
3. today I do have to no work more.
I have no more work to do today.
4. nowhere play is us ball There for to.
There is nowhere for us to play ball.
5. complains leg about never her She broken.
She never complains about her broken leg.
6. ridden ever horse Jeremy a hasn't.
Jeremy hasn't ever ridden a horse.

109

Page 110

Match the definitions below to a word in the Word Bank. Find and circle the words in the puzzle. The first one has been done for you.

FACTOID — The smallest frogs in the world are about one centimeter long. Now that's tiny!

1. ABC order
2. not a vowel
3. more than one
4. names things
5. mark used for stress
6. part of a word
7. describes nouns
8. used in place of a noun
9. just one
10. added to the beginning of a base word
11. describes verbs
12. not a consonant
13. added to the end of a base word
14. shows action

Word Bank
12 vowel
3 plural
6 syllable
1 alphabetical
2 consonant
10 prefix
7 adjectives
4 nouns
14 verb
13 suffix
8 pronoun
11 adverbs
5 accent
9 singular

110

Better Bodies · Better Behavior

Up until now, **Summer Bridge Activities**™ has been all about your mind...

But the other parts of you—who you are, how you act, and how you feel—are important too. These pages are all about helping build a better you this summer.

Keeping your body strong and healthy helps you live better, learn better, and feel better. To keep your body healthy, you need to do things like eat right, get enough sleep, and exercise. The Physical Fitness pages of Building Better Bodies will teach you about good eating habits and the importance of proper exercise. You can even train for a Presidential Fitness Award over the summer.

The Character pages are all about building a better you on the inside. They've got fun activities for you and your family to do together. The activities will help you develop important values and habits you'll need as you grow up.

After a summer of Building Better Bodies and Behavior and **Summer Bridge Activities**™, there may be a whole new you ready for school in the fall!

For Parents: Introduction to Character Education

Character education is simply giving your child clear messages about the values you and your family consider important. Many studies have shown that a basic core of values is universal. You will find certain values reflected in the laws of every country and incorporated in the teachings of religious, ethical, and other belief systems throughout the world.

The character activities included here are designed to span the entire summer. Each week your child will be introduced to a new value, with a quote and two activities that illustrate it. Research has shown that character education is most effective when parents reinforce the values in their child's daily routine; therefore, we encourage parents to be involved as their child completes the lessons.

Here are some suggestions on how to maximize these lessons.
- Read through the lesson yourself. Then set aside a block of time for you and your child to discuss the value.
- Plan a block of time to work on the suggested activities.
- Discuss the meaning of the quote with your child. Ask, "What do you think the quote means?" Have your child ask other members of the family the same question. If possible, include grandparents, aunts, uncles, and cousins.
- Use the quote as often as you can during the week. You'll be pleasantly surprised to learn that both you and your child will have it memorized by the end of the week.
- For extra motivation, you can set a reward for completing each week's activities.
- Point out to your child other people who are actively displaying a value. Example: "See how John is helping Mrs. Olsen by raking her leaves."
- Be sure to praise your child each time he or she practices a value: "Mary, it was very courteous of you to wait until I finished speaking."
- Find time in your day to talk about values. Turn off the radio in the car and chat with your children; take a walk in the evening as a family; read a story about the weekly value at bedtime; or give a back rub while you talk about what makes your child happy or sad.
- Finally, model the values you want your child to acquire. Remember, children will do as you do, not as you say.

Name _____ Date _____

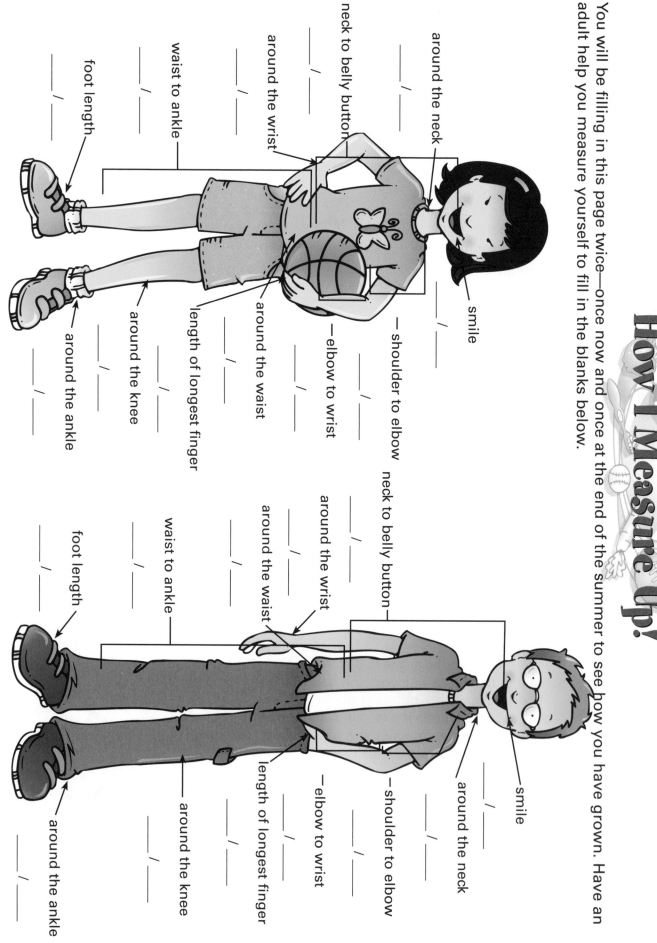

How I Measure Up!

You will be filling in this page twice—once now and once at the end of the summer to see how you have grown. Have an adult help you measure yourself to fill in the blanks below.

around the neck ___/___

neck to belly button ___/___

around the wrist ___/___

waist to ankle ___/___

foot length ___/___

smile ___/___

shoulder to elbow ___/___

elbow to wrist ___/___

around the waist ___/___

length of longest finger ___/___

around the knee ___/___

around the ankle ___/___

around the neck ___/___

neck to belly button ___/___

around the wrist ___/___

waist to ankle ___/___

foot length ___/___

smile ___/___

shoulder to elbow ___/___

elbow to wrist ___/___

around the waist ___/___

length of longest finger ___/___

around the knee ___/___

around the ankle ___/___

Nutrition

The food you eat helps your body grow. It gives you energy to work and play. Some foods give you protein or fats. Other foods provide vitamins, minerals, or carbohydrates. These are all things your body needs. Eating a variety of good foods each day will help you stay healthy. How much and what foods you need depends on many things, including whether you're a girl or boy, how active you are, and how old you are. To figure out the right amount of food for you, go to http://www.mypyramid.gov/mypyramid/index.aspx and use the Pyramid Plan Calculator. In the meantime, here are some general guidelines.

Your body needs nutrients from each food group every day.

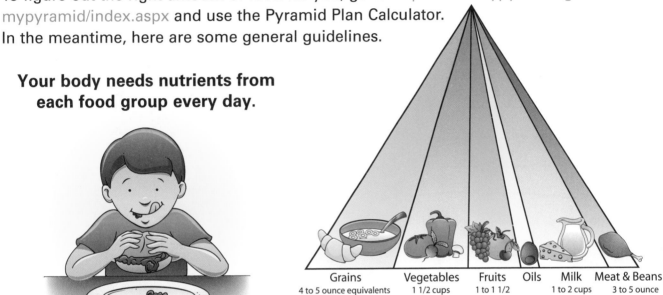

Grains	Vegetables	Fruits	Oils	Milk	Meat & Beans
4 to 5 ounce equivalents each day (an ounce might be a slice of bread, a packet of oatmeal, or a bowl of cereal)	1 1/2 cups each day	1 to 1 1/2 cups each day		1 to 2 cups of milk (or other calcium-rich food) each day	3 to 5 ounce equivalents each day

What foods did you eat today?

Which food group did you eat the most foods from today?

From which food group did you eat the least?

Which meal included the most food groups?

Meal Planning

Plan out three balanced meals for one day. Arrange your meals so that by the end of the day, you will have had all the recommended amounts of food from each food group listed on the food pyramid.

Breakfast

Lunch

Dinner

Meal Tracker

Use these charts to record the amount of food you eat from each food group for one or two weeks. Have another family member keep track, too, and compare.

	Grains	Milk	Meat & Beans	Fruits	Vegetables	Oils/ Sweets
Monday						
Tuesday						
Wednesday						
Thursday						
Friday						
Saturday						
Sunday						

	Grains	Milk	Meat & Beans	Fruits	Vegetables	Oils/ Sweets
Monday						
Tuesday						
Wednesday						
Thursday						
Friday						
Saturday						
Sunday						

	Grains	Milk	Meat & Beans	Fruits	Vegetables	Oils/ Sweets
Monday						
Tuesday						
Wednesday						
Thursday						
Friday						
Saturday						
Sunday						

	Grains	Milk	Meat & Beans	Fruits	Vegetables	Oils/ Sweets
Monday						
Tuesday						
Wednesday						
Thursday						
Friday						
Saturday						
Sunday						

Get Moving!

Did you know that getting no exercise can be almost as bad for you as smoking? So get moving this summer!

Summer is the perfect time to get out and get in shape. Your fitness program should include three parts:

- Get 30 minutes of aerobic exercise per day, three to five days a week.

- Exercise your muscles to improve strength and flexibility.

- Make it FUN! Do things that you like to do. Include your friends and family.

Aerobic

Strength & Flexibility

Fun

If the time you spend on activities 4 and 5 adds up to more than you spend on 1–3, you could be headed for a spud's life!

Couch Potato Quiz

1. Name three things you do each day that get you moving.

2. Name three things you do a few times a week that are good exercise.

3. How many hours do you spend each week playing outside or exercising?

4. How much TV do you watch each day?

5. How much time do you spend playing computer or video games?

**You can find information on fitness at
www.fitness.gov or www.kidshealth.org**

Activity Pyramid

The Activity Pyramid works like the Food Pyramid. You can use the Activity Pyramid to help plan your summer exercise program. Fill in the blanks below.

List 1 thing that isn't good exercise that you could do less of this summer.

1._____

List 3 fun activities you enjoy that get you moving and are good exercise.

1._____

2._____

3._____

List 3 exercises you could do to build strength and flexibility this summer.

1._____

2._____

3._____

Cut Down On

TV time
video or computer games
sitting for more than
30 minutes at a time

2–3 Times a Week

Work & Play
bowling
swinging
fishing
jump rope
yard work

Strength & Stretching
dancing
martial arts
gymnastics
push-ups/pull-ups

List 3 activities you would like to do for aerobic exercise this summer.

1._____

2._____

3._____

List 2 sports you would like to participate in this summer.

1._____

2._____

3–5 Times a Week
at least 30 minutes

Aerobic Exercise
walking   skating
running   bicycling
swimming

Sports/Recreation
soccer   relay races
basketball   tennis
volleyball   baseball

Every Day

walk
play outside
take the stairs
bathe your pet

help with chores:
sweeping
washing dishes
picking up
clothes and toys

Adapted from the President's Council on Fitness and Sports

List 5 everyday things you can do to get moving more often.

1._____

2._____

3._____

4._____

5._____

Fitness Fundamentals

Basic physical fitness includes several things:

Cardiovascular Endurance. Your cardiovascular system includes your heart and blood vessels. You need a strong heart to pump your blood which delivers oxygen and nutrients to your body.

Muscular Strength. This is how strong your muscles are.

Muscular Endurance. Endurance has to do with how long you can use your muscles before they get tired.

Flexibility. This is your ability to move your joints and to use your muscles through their full range of motion.

Body Composition. Your body is made up of lean mass and fat mass.

Lean mass includes the water, muscles, tissues, and organs in your body.

Fat mass includes the fat your body stores for energy. Exercise helps you burn body fat and maintain good body composition.

The goal of a summer fitness program is to improve in all the areas of physical fitness.

You build cardiovascular endurance through **aerobic** exercise. For **aerobic** exercise, you need to work large muscle groups at a steady pace. This increases your heart rate and breathing. You can jog, walk, hike, swim, dance, do aerobics, ride a bike, go rowing, climb stairs, rollerblade, play golf, backpack...

You should get at least 30 minutes of aerobic exercise per day, three to five days a week.

You build muscular strength and endurance with exercises that work your muscles, like sit-ups, push-ups, pull-ups, and weight lifting.

You can increase flexibility through stretching exercises. These are good for warm-ups, too.

Find these fitness words.

Word Bank		
aerobic	exercise	fat
muscular	flexible	blood
endurance	strength	oxygen
heart rate	joint	hiking

```
u a e y i d t y a g d x p o b
o l s h s t r e n g t h l r c
e w l o o o z v s d m i h d t
g t z w s j o i n t m n k a o
s q a c h i p s a d e t f f m
k c q r x i q f l e x i b l e
e e j o t v k w t e u r g e g
i e s e d r v i n t n f k x o
k e l i d c a d n n e g e j w
u z e d c y u e i g g x i c i
j c i b o r e a h h y w v s i
a m r a a c e m x x x y d i g
f p v n p n d x u s o x e f k
p o c b l o o d e g z a x m c
l e m u s c u l a r m k g i s
```

Your Summer Fitness Program

Start your summer fitness program by choosing at least one aerobic activity from your Activity Pyramid. You can choose more than one for variety.

_____   _____   _____

Do this activity three to five times each week. Keep it up for at least 30 minutes each time.
(Exercise hard enough to increase your heart rate and your breathing. Don't exercise so hard that you get dizzy or can't catch your breath.)

Use this chart to plan when you will exercise, or use it as a record when you exercise.

DATE	ACTIVITY	TIME

DATE	ACTIVITY	TIME

Plan a reward for meeting your exercise goals for two weeks.
(You can make copies of this chart to track your fitness all summer long.)

Start Slow!

Remember to start out slow. Exercise is about getting stronger. It's not about being superman—or superwoman—right off the bat.

Are You Up to the Challenge?

The Presidential Physical Fitness Award Program was designed to help kids get into shape and have fun. To earn the award, you take five fitness tests. These are usually given by teachers at school, but you can train for them this summer. Make a chart to track your progress. Keep working all summer to see if you can improve your score.

Remember: Start Slow!

1. Curl-ups. Lie on the floor with your knees bent and your feet about 12 inches from your buttocks. Cross your arms over your chest. Raise your trunk up and touch your elbows to your thighs. Do as many as you can in one minute.

2. Shuttle Run. Draw a starting line. Put two blocks 30 feet away. Run the 30 feet, pick up a block, and bring it back to the starting line. Then run and bring back the second block. Record your fastest time.

3. V-sit Reach. Sit on the floor with your legs straight and your feet 8 to 12 inches apart. Put a ruler between your feet, pointing past your toes. Have a partner hold your legs straight, and keep your toes pointed up. Link your thumbs together and reach forward, palms down, as far as you can along the ruler.

4. One-Mile Walk/Run. On a track or some safe area, run one mile. You can walk as often as you need to. Finish as fast as possible. (Ages six to seven may want to run a quarter mile; ages eight to nine, half a mile.)

5. Pull-ups. Grip a bar with an overhand grip (the backs of your hands toward your face). Have someone lift you up if you need help. Hang with your arms and legs straight. Pull your body up until your chin is over the bar; then let yourself back down. Do as many as you can.

Respect

Respect is showing good manners toward all people, not just those you know or who are like you. Respect is treating everyone, no matter what religion, race, or culture, male or female, rich or poor, in a way that you would want to be treated. The easiest way to do this is to decide to **never** take part in activities and to **never** use words that make fun of people because they are different from you or your friends.

It's not necessary for eagles to be crows. What I am, I am.
~ Sitting Bull

Word Search

Find these words that also mean *respect*.

Word Bank

honor
idolize
admire
worship
recognize
appreciate
venerate
prize

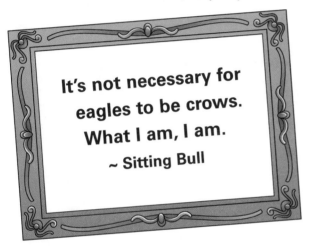

```
m c e t a r e n e v
w j t a h p s e p t
e c a d n n t z i w
z v i m w u k i h r
i e c i h b h n s o
l z e r v b j g r n
o i r e k a u o o o
d r p g m e e c w h
i p p b g c h e r j
q f a b f g u r r z
```

Activity

This week go to the library and check out *The Well: David's Story* by Mildred Taylor (1995). The story is set in Mississippi in the early 1900s and tells about David's family, who shares their well with both black and white neighbors. Be sure to read this book with your parents.

Gratitude

Gratitude is when you thank people for the good things they have given you or done for you. Thinking about people and events in your life that make you feel grateful (thankful) will help you become a happier person.

There are over 465 different ways of saying thank you. Here are a few:

Danke   Toda   Merci   Gracias   **Nandri**

Spasibo   Arigato   **Gadda ge**   Paldies   Hvala

Make a list of ten things you are grateful for.

1. _____
2. _____
3. _____
4. _____
5. _____

6. _____
7. _____
8. _____
9. _____
10. _____

A Recipe for Saying Thanks

1. Make a colorful card.
2. On the inside, write a thank-you note to someone who has done something nice for you.
3. Address an envelope to that person.
4. Pick out a cool stamp.
5. Drop your note in the nearest mailbox.

Saying thank you creates love.
~ Daphne Rose Kingma

Manners

If you were the only person in the world, you wouldn't have to have **good manners** or be **courteous**. However, there are over six billion people on our planet, and good manners help us all get along with each other.

Children with good manners are usually well liked by other children and are certainly liked by adults. Here are some simple rules for good manners:

- When you ask for something, say, "Please."
- When someone gives you something, say, "Thank you."
- When someone says, "Thank you," say, "You're welcome."
- If you walk in front of someone or bump into a person, say, "Excuse me."
- When someone else is talking, wait before speaking.
- Share and take turns.

No kindness, no matter how small, is ever wasted. ~ Aesop's Fables

Find these words or phrases that deal with *courtesy*.

Word Bank
etiquette
thank you
welcome
excuse me
please
share
turns
patience
polite
manners

```
m u o y k n a h t
e m o c l e w e e
e s a e l p x f c
a m q u f c x r n
e t t e u q i t e
s r g s n r u t i
s r e n n a m g t
v m p o l i t e a
e i e r a h s h p
```

I've Got Manners

Make a colorful poster to display on your bedroom door or on the refrigerator. List five ways you are going to practice your manners. Be creative and decorate with watercolors, poster paints, pictures cut from magazines, clip art, or geometric shapes.

Instead of making a poster, you could make a mobile to hang from your ceiling that shows five different manners to practice.

Consequences

A **consequence** is what happens after you choose to do something. Some choices lead to good consequences. Other choices lead to bad consequences. An example of this would be choosing whether to eat an apple or a bag of potato chips. The potato chips might seem like a more tasty snack, but eating an apple is better for your body. Or, you may not like to do your homework, but if you choose not to, you won't do well in school, and you may not be able to go out with your friends.

It's hard to look into the future and see how a choice will influence what happens today, tomorrow, or years from now. But whenever we choose to do something, there are consequences that go with our choice. That's why it is important to *think before you choose.*

Remember: The easiest choice does not always lead to the best consequence.

> We choose to go to the moon not because it's easy, but because it's hard.
> ~ John F. Kennedy

Activity

Get a copy of *The Tale of Peter Rabbit* by Beatrix Potter. This simple story is full of choices that lead to bad consequences. Write down three choices Peter made and the consequences that occurred. Who made a good choice, and what was the consequence?

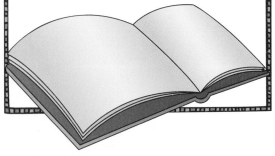

Find these words that also mean *consequence.*

Word Bank		
result	outcome	fallout
payoff	effect	reaction
product	aftermath	upshot

b	e	h	p	j	c	p	o	j	q
i	t	h	a	e	l	r	w	r	v
z	u	t	y	f	r	o	s	t	v
g	o	a	o	f	e	d	t	o	m
r	l	m	f	e	a	u	r	h	j
e	l	r	f	c	c	c	e	s	e
s	a	e	b	t	t	t	m	p	g
u	f	t	s	e	i	j	t	u	i
l	e	f	e	m	o	c	t	u	o
t	c	a	i	m	n	o	h	f	d

Friendship

Friends come in all sizes, shapes, and ages: brothers, sisters, parents, neighbors, good teachers, and school and sports friends.

There is a saying, "To have a friend you need to be a friend." Can you think of a day when someone might have tried to get you to say or do unkind things to someone else? Sometimes it takes courage to be a real friend. Did you have the courage to say no?

A Recipe for Friendship

1 cup of always listening to ideas and stories
2 pounds of never talking behind a friend's back
1 pound of no mean teasing
2 cups of always helping a friend who needs help

Take these ingredients and mix completely together. Add laughter, kindness, hugs, and even tears. Bake for as long as it takes to make your friendship good and strong.

I get by with a little help from my friends.

~ John Lennon

Family Night at the Movies

Rent *Toy Story* or *Toy Story II*. Each movie is a simple, yet powerful, tale about true friendship. Fix a big bowl of popcorn to share with your family during the show.

International Friendship Day

The first Sunday in August is International Friendship Day. This is a perfect day to remember all your friends and how they have helped you during your friendship. Give your friends a call or send them an email or snail-mail card.

Confidence

People are **confident** or have **confidence** when they feel like they can succeed at a certain task. To feel confident about doing something, most people need to practice a task over and over.

Reading, pitching a baseball, writing in cursive, playing the flute, even mopping a floor are all examples of tasks that need to be practiced before people feel confident they can succeed.

What are five things you feel confident doing?

What is one thing you want to feel more confident doing?

Make a plan for how and when you will practice until you feel confident.

You Crack Me Up!

Materials needed:
1 dozen eggs
a mixing bowl

Cracking eggs without breaking the yolk or getting egg whites all over your hands takes practice.

1. Watch an adult break an egg into the bowl. How did they hold their hands? How did they pull the egg apart?

2. Now you try. Did you do a perfect job the first time? Keep trying until you begin to feel confident about cracking eggs.

3. Use the eggs immediately to make a cheese omelet or custard pie. Refrigerate any unused eggs for up to three days.

Pride

Never bend your head.

Always hold it high.

Look the world

Right in the eye.

~ Helen Keller

Responsibility

You show **responsibility** by doing what you agree or promise to do. It might be a task, such as a homework assignment, or a chore, such as feeding your fish.

When you are young, your parents and teachers will give you simple tasks like putting away toys or brushing your teeth without being asked. As you get older, you will be given more responsibility. You might be trusted to come home from a friend's house at a certain time or drive to the store for groceries.

It takes a lot of practice to grow up to be a responsible person. The easiest way to practice is by keeping your promises and doing what you know is right.

A parent is responsible for different things than a child or a teenager. Write three activities you are responsible for every day. Then write three things a parent is responsible for every day.

If you want your eggs hatched, sit on them yourself. ~ Haitian Proverb

Activity

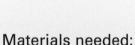

Materials needed:
21 pennies or counters such as beans, rocks, or marbles
2 small containers labeled #1 and #2

Decide on a reward for successfully completing this activity.
Put all the counters in container #1.
Review the three activities you are responsible for every day.
Each night before you go to bed, put one counter for each completed activity into container #2. At the end of seven days count all the counters in container #2.
If you have 16 or more counters in container #2, you are on your way to becoming very responsible. Collect your reward.

My reward is_____.

Service/Helping

Service is **helping** another person or group of people without asking for any kind of reward or payment. These are some good things that happen when you do service:

1. You feel closer to the people in your community (neighborhood).
2. You feel pride in yourself when you see that you can help other people in need.
3. Your family feels proud of you.
4. You will make new friends as you help others.

An old saying goes, "Charity begins at home." This means that you don't have to do big, important-sounding things to help people. You can start in your own home and neighborhood.

Activity

Each day this week, do one act of service around your house. Don't ask for or take any kind of payment or reward. Be creative! Possible acts of service are

1. Carry in the groceries, do the dishes, or fold the laundry.
2. Read aloud to a younger brother or sister.
3. Make breakfast or pack lunches.
4. Recycle newspapers and cans.
5. Clean the refrigerator or your room.

At the end of the week, think of a project to do with your family that will help your community. You could play musical instruments or sing at a nursing home, set up a lemonade stand and give the money you make to the Special Olympics, offer to play board games with children in the hospital, or pick some flowers and take them to a neighbor. The list goes on and on.

> **All the flowers of tomorrow are in the seeds of today.**
> ~ Indian Proverb

Word Search

Find these words that also mean *service*.

Word Bank		
help	assist	aid
charity	support	boost
benefit	contribute	guide

```
m v l a o d w f d r
c o n t r i b u t e
t b s x c a z v x q
s g p q g w b n y t
i v l y g u v x z i
s n e t e x m n m f
s f h d u d g t e e
a u c h a r i t y n
s u p p o r t u x e
b o o s t g f j g b
```

Honesty and Trust

Being an **honest** person means you don't steal, cheat, or tell lies. **Trust** is when you believe someone will be honest. If you are dishonest, or not truthful, people will not trust you.

You want to tell the truth because it is important to have your family and friends trust you. However, it takes courage to tell the truth, especially if you don't want people to get mad at you or be disappointed in the way you behaved.

How would your parents feel if you lied to them? People almost always find out about lies, and most parents will be more angry about a lie than if you had told them the truth in the first place.

When family or friends ask about something, remember that honesty is telling the truth. Honesty is telling what really happened. Honesty is keeping your promises. *Be proud of being an honest person.*

Write down five feeling words about how you felt when you *weren't* honest or trusted.

Write down five feeling words about how you felt when you *were* honest or trusted.

1.
2.
3.
4.
5.

Parent note: Help your child by pointing out times he or she acted honestly.

Count to Ten

Tape ten pieces of colored paper to your refrigerator. For one week, each time you tell the truth or keep a promise, take one piece of paper down and put it in the recycling bin. If all ten pieces of paper are gone by the end of the week, collect your reward.

Most Improved

Honesty is the first chapter in the book of wisdom.
~Thomas Jefferson

My reward is_____.

Happiness

Happiness is a feeling that comes when you enjoy your life. Different things make different people happy. Some people feel happy when they are playing soccer. Other people feel happy when they are playing the cello. It is important to understand what makes you happy so you can include some of these things in your daily plan.

These are some actions that show you are happy: laughing, giggling, skipping, smiling, and hugging.

Make a list of five activities that make you feel happy.

1.
2.
3.
4.
5.

Bonus!

List two things you could do to make someone else happy.

1._____

2._____

Activity

Write down a plan to do one activity each day this week that makes you happy.

Try simple things—listen to your favorite song, play with a friend, bake muffins, shoot hoops, etc.

Be sure to thank everyone who helps you, and don't forget to laugh!

Happy Thought

The world is so full

of a number of things,

I'm sure we should

all be happy as kings.

~Robert Louis Stevenson

Notes

_____

_____

_____

_____

_____

_____

_____

_____

_____

_____

_____

_____

_____

_____

_____

_____

_____

_____

5 Five things I'm thankful for:

1. _____

2. _____

3. _____

4. _____

5. _____

Notes

_____

_____

_____

_____

_____

_____

_____

_____

_____

_____

_____

_____

_____

_____

_____

_____

_____

_____

_____

Five things I'm thankful for:

5

1. _____

2. _____

3. _____

4. _____

5. _____

Multiplication and Division

Developing multiplication and division math skills can be a challenging experience for both parent and child.

- **Have a positive attitude.**
- **Relax and enjoy the learning process.**
- **Keep the learning time short and fun you will get better results.**
- **Review the cards with your child.**
- **Read the front of the card.**
- **Check your answer on the reverse side.**
- **Separate those he/she does not know.**
- **Review those he/she does know.**
- **Gradually work through the other cards.**

These steps will help build your child's confidence with multiplication and division. Enjoy the rewards!

"Teacher, Teacher"

Three or more players.
Each player takes a turn as "Teacher."
The Teacher mixes up the flashcards and holds one card up at a time.
First player to yell out "Teacher, Teacher,"
will have the first chance to give the answer.
If his/her answer is right he/she receives 5 points.
If his/her answer is wrong, he/she will not receive any points.
Move on to the next person until someone answers correctly.
The next round someone else is teacher.
Repeat each round.
Reward the different levels, everyone wins!

Time Challenge

Follow the directions for "Teacher, Teacher" and add a time to it.
Increase the point system to meet the Time Challenge.
Reward the different levels, everyone wins!

0	0	0	0
x 0	x 1	x 2	x 3
4	3	2	1

0	0	0	0
x 4	x 5	x 6	x 7
8	7	6	5

0	0	0	1
x 8	x 9	x 10	x 1
3	2	1	9

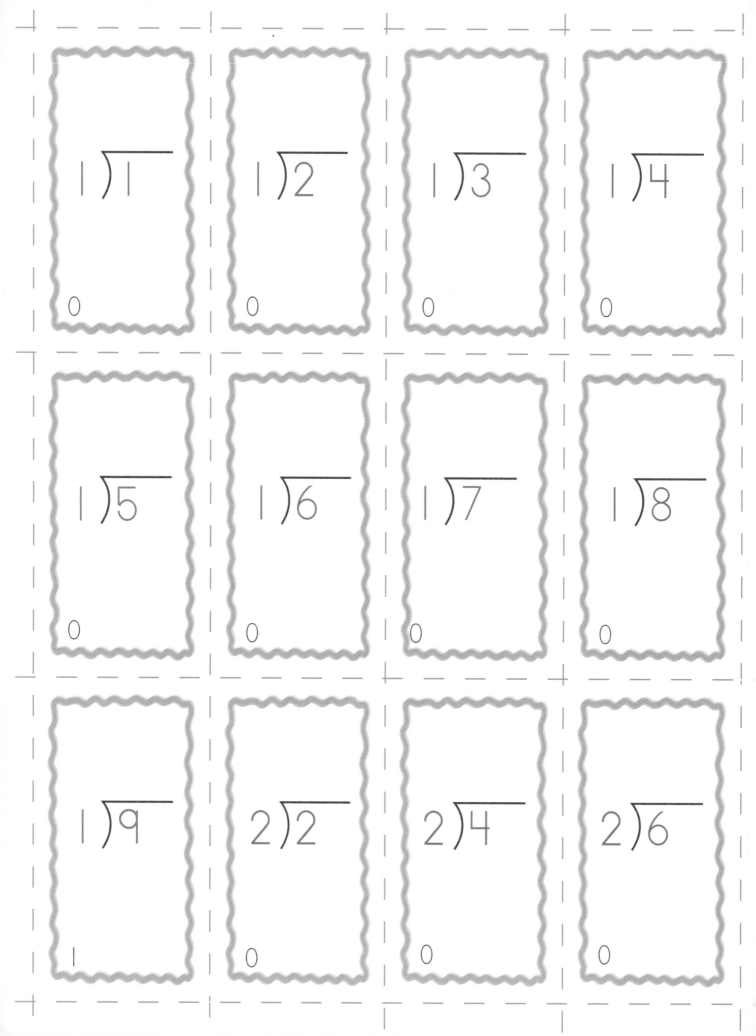

$1\overline{)1}$

0

$1\overline{)2}$

0

$1\overline{)3}$

0

$1\overline{)4}$

0

$1\overline{)5}$

0

$1\overline{)6}$

0

$1\overline{)7}$

0

$1\overline{)8}$

0

$1\overline{)9}$

1

$2\overline{)2}$

0

$2\overline{)4}$

0

$2\overline{)6}$

0

2 x 1 ——— 7	2 x 2 ——— 6	3 x 1 ——— 5	3 x 2 ——— 4
3 x 3 ——— 2	4 x 1 ——— 1	4 x 2 ——— 9	4 x 3 ——— 8
4 x 4 ——— 6	5 x 1 ——— 5	5 x 2 ——— 4	5 x 3 ——— 3

$2\overline{)8}$	$2\overline{)10}$	$2\overline{)12}$	$2\overline{)14}$
6	3	4	2

$2\overline{)16}$	$2\overline{)18}$	$3\overline{)3}$	$3\overline{)6}$
12	8	4	9

$3\overline{)9}$	$3\overline{)12}$	$3\overline{)15}$	$3\overline{)18}$
15	10	5	16

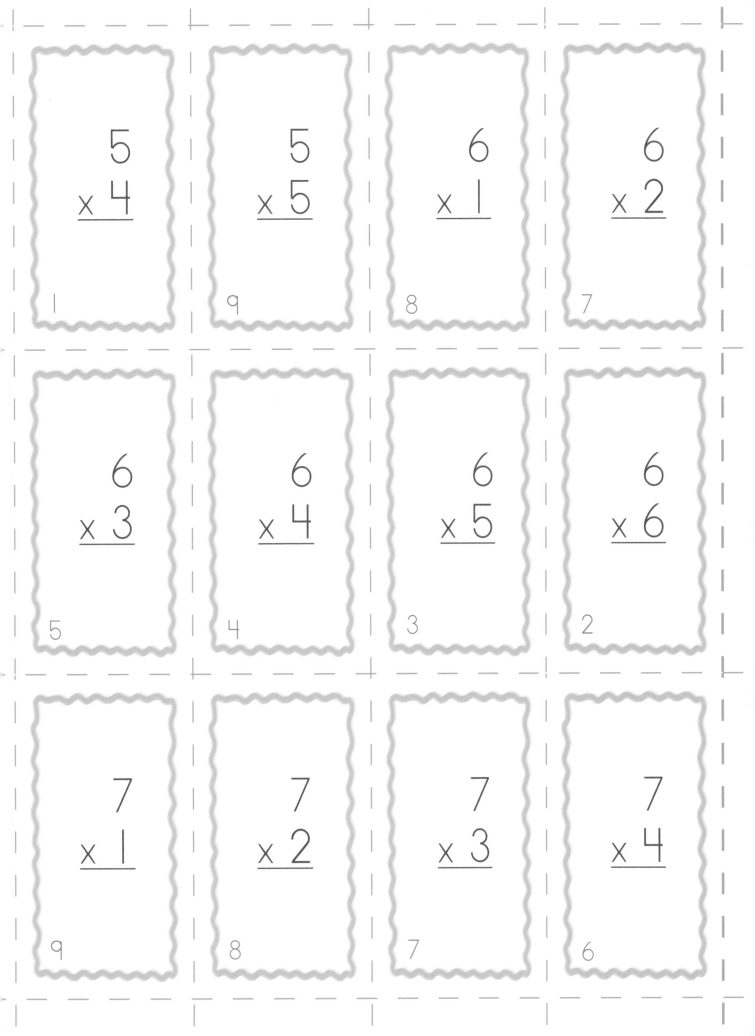

| | 5
x 4 | 5
x 5 | 6
x 1 | 6
x 2 |
| | 1 | 9 | 8 | 7 |

6
x 3
5

6
x 4
4

6
x 5
3

6
x 6
2

7
x 1
9

7
x 2
8

7
x 3
7

7
x 4
6

$3\overline{)21}$	$3\overline{)24}$	$3\overline{)27}$	$4\overline{)4}$
12	6	25	20

$4\overline{)8}$	$4\overline{)12}$	$4\overline{)16}$	$4\overline{)20}$
36	30	24	18

$4\overline{)24}$	$4\overline{)28}$	$4\overline{)32}$	$4\overline{)36}$
28	21	14	7

7 x 5 4	7 x 6 3	7 x 7 2	8 x 1 1
8 x 2 8	8 x 3 7	8 x 4 6	8 x 5 5
8 x 6 3	8 x 7 2	8 x 8 1	9 x 1 9

$5\overline{)5}$	$5\overline{)10}$	$5\overline{)15}$	$5\overline{)20}$
8	49	42	35

$5\overline{)25}$	$5\overline{)30}$	$5\overline{)35}$	$5\overline{)40}$
40	32	24	16

$5\overline{)45}$	$6\overline{)6}$	$6\overline{)12}$	$6\overline{)18}$
9	64	56	48

9 x 2 — 7	9 x 3 — 6	9 x 4 — 5	9 x 5 — 4
9 x 6 — 2	9 x 7 — 1	9 x 8 — 9	9 x 9 — 8
10 x 1 — 6	10 x 2 — 5	10 x 3 — 4	10 x 4 — 3

$6 \overline{)24}$	$6 \overline{)30}$	$6 \overline{)36}$	$6 \overline{)42}$
45	36	27	18

$6 \overline{)48}$	$6 \overline{)54}$	$7 \overline{)7}$	$7 \overline{)14}$
81	72	63	54

$7 \overline{)21}$	$7 \overline{)28}$	$7 \overline{)35}$	$7 \overline{)42}$
40	30	20	10

10
x 5
7

10
x 6
6

10
x 7
5

10
x 8
4

10
x 9
2

10
x 10
1

7)49
9

7)56
8

7)63
6

8)8
5

8)16
4

8)24
3

$8\overline{)32}$

80

$8\overline{)40}$

70

$8\overline{)48}$

60

$8\overline{)56}$

50

$8\overline{)64}$

8

$8\overline{)72}$

7

$9\overline{)9}$

100

$9\overline{)18}$

90

$9\overline{)27}$

3

$9\overline{)36}$

2

$9\overline{)45}$

1

$9\overline{)54}$

9

$9\overline{)63}$

$9\overline{)72}$

$9\overline{)81}$

$10\overline{)10}$

0

0

0

0

$10\overline{)20}$

$10\overline{)30}$

$10\overline{)40}$

$10\overline{)50}$

0

0

0

0

$10\overline{)60}$

$10\overline{)70}$

$10\overline{)80}$

$10\overline{)90}$

0

0

$1 \overline{)0}$

1

$2 \overline{)0}$

9

$3 \overline{)0}$

8

$4 \overline{)0}$

7

$5 \overline{)0}$

5

$6 \overline{)0}$

4

$7 \overline{)0}$

3

$8 \overline{)0}$

2

$9 \overline{)0}$

9

$10 \overline{)0}$

8

7

6

Congratulations!

your name

HAS COMPLETED

Summer Bridge Activities™

AND IS READY FOR THE 5TH GRADE!

Ms. Hansen

Ms. Hansen

Mr. Fredrickson

Mr. Fredrickson

Parent's Signature

WWW.SUMMER BRIDGE ACTIVITIES.COM